T0267297

# THE

# REMOTE
# WORKER'S

## HANDBOOK

### HOW TO WORK

# EFFECTIVELY

### from

# ANYWHERE

THE STAFF OF ENTREPRENEUR MEDIA
AND JASON R. RICH

Entrepreneur Press®

Entrepreneur Press, Publisher
Cover Design: Andrew Welyczko
Production and Composition: Eliot House Productions

© 2023 by Entrepreneur Media, Inc.
All rights reserved.
Reproduction or translation of any part of this work beyond that permitted by Section
107 or 108 of the 1976 United States Copyright Act without permission of the copyright
owner is unlawful. Requests for permission or further information should be addressed
to Entrepreneur Media, Inc. Attn: Legal Department, 18061 Fitch, Irvine, CA 92614.

This publication is designed to provide accurate and authoritative information
in regard to the subject matter covered. It is sold with the understanding that the
publisher is not engaged in rendering legal, accounting, or other professional services.
If legal advice or other expert assistance is required, the services of a competent
professional person should be sought.

Entrepreneur Press® is a registered trademark of Entrepreneur Media, Inc.

**Library of Congress Cataloging-in-Publication Data**
Names: Rich, Jason, author. | Entrepreneur Media, Inc., issuing body.
Title: The remote worker's handbook: how to work effectively from anywhere / by
   The Staff of Entrepreneur Media, Jason R. Rich.
Description: Irvine: Entrepreneur Press, [2023] | Includes index. | Summary: "As more
   traditional businesses rethink the evolving work space, adapting is imperative for
   the successful remote worker. Whether a seasoned professional or fresh on the
   scene, The Remote Worker's Handbook gives you the tools to harness an entirely
   new skill set for a seamless passage into the modern employment frontier."—
   Provided by publisher.
Identifiers: LCCN 2022047259 | ISBN 9781642011562 (trade paperback) |
   ISBN 9781613084663 (epub)
Subjects: LCSH: Telecommuting. | Virtual work teams. Classification: LCC
   HD2336.3 .R53 2023 | DDC 658.3/123--dc23/eng/20220930
LC record available at https://lccn.loc.gov/2022047259

Printed in the United States of America

26  25  24  23                                                    10 9 8 7 6 5 4 3 2 1

# Contents

## CHAPTER 5

## Work Successfully from a Shared Work Space . . . . . . . 91

## CHAPTER 6

## How to Remotely Collaborate . . . . . . . . . . . . . . . . . . . . 101

## CHAPTER 7

## Working with PDF Files Instead of Paper Files . . . . . . . 117

## CHAPTER 8

### Effectively Deal with Online Security
### and Privacy Issues . . . . . . . . . . . . . . . . . . . . . . . . . . . . . **129**

## CHAPTER 9

### 25 Strategies for Hosting and
### Participating in Effective Virtual Meetings . . . . . . . . **147**

CHAPTER 10

## The Psychological Aspect of Working Remotely. . . . . 167

# Introduction

Prior to COVID-19, only about 5.7 million people in the United States were considered "remote workers," according to workplace research and consulting firm Global Workplace Analytics. However, when COVID-19 was officially declared a pandemic in March 2020, everything changed quickly. By the end of the year, Pew Research reported that 71 percent of American workers who said their jobs could be done remotely were in fact working from home.

By 2022, while the United States and most other countries continued to grapple with COVID-19, many people returned to their office jobs, but an unprecedented number of people across a wide range of industries (such as health care, technology, and financial services) continued to work remotely, and this is not likely to change.

In fact, freelancing platform Upwork estimated in its 2020 "Future Workforce Pulse Report" that by 2025, 22 percent of the entire U.S. work-force (approximately 36.2 million Americans) will be working remotely. This means that more employers than ever before will offer remote work as a viable (and sometimes preferred) option for their employees.

We've already seen that traditional offices for established businesses are being shut down. According to the 2021 "State of Remote Work" report by Owl Labs, 16 percent of companies around the world now oper-ate fully remotely. This represents one of the biggest changes in how busi-nesses operate since the Industrial Revolution back in the 1800s.

Countless people who once worked in a traditional office setting, either by employer mandate or by choice, have abandoned their offices or cubicles to work remotely, either from home or another location. These people, and you may be one of them, must relearn how to do their jobs while relying much more than ever before on technology. Remote workers need to acquire an entirely new skill set, alter their workflow, and adapt their mentality to successfully handle their professional responsibilities and communicate and collaborate with their employer, co-workers, cus-tomers, and clients.

So as people around the world talk about a "return to normal" as COVID-19 becomes less of an immediate threat to our health, for many of us this means a permanent "new normal" that includes remote work. This already represents an 87 percent increase in remote workers around the globe, compared to prepandemic levels.

## What It Means to Work Remotely

Working remotely does not necessarily mean working from home. It refers to someone who works outside a traditional office operated by their employer, either on a full-time or hybrid basis (meaning that at least one day per week, they do their job outside a traditional office). While this might very well mean working from home, it could also mean working from a shared work space, a coffee shop, a hotel room, an airport, or even a car.

Thanks to new technologies and many companies' recent efforts to adapt, a growing number of people in a wide range of industries can now perform their job from virtually anywhere. However, this often means abandoning the status quo and adopting new ways to communicate, collaborate, stay organized, stay motivated, and handle time management and scheduling while remaining as productive as ever—even when not under direct supervision.

*The Remote Worker's Handbook* is your comprehensive roadmap for navigating the fast-evolving remote work frontier. This book will help you understand the pros and cons of working remotely, teach you how to overcome the many new professional challenges you'll face, harness the power of the technologies at your disposal, establish a well-equipped home office or remote work space, and deal with the psychological aspects of working outside a traditional office.

As you're about to discover, no matter how experienced and skilled you are at your job, becoming a successful remote worker will require you to learn and master an entirely new skill set that relies heavily on technology. Yes, this can be intimidating, but remember that millions of people were working remotely long before the COVID-19 pandemic. They already knew what you will soon discover: being a remote worker has some significant advantages and perks, which we will explore throughout this book.

There are, however, also some common pitfalls related to remote work. With the help of this book, you can learn to avoid them and save yourself time, money, stress, and aggravation, even if your employer does not provide you with the training and guidance you need to adapt to a remote work situation.

HR technology firm Quantum Workplace's 2021 report "The State of Remote Work," for example, shows that remote and hybrid workers have higher levels of engagement than people doing similar jobs from a traditional office, and both they and their employers agree shifting to remote work has had no negative effect on their productivity.

Meanwhile, according to social media management company Buffer's 2022 "State of Remote Work" report, 97 percent of remote professionals would recommend working remotely to others, and 97 percent of those who worked remotely during COVID-19 would, if given the choice, continue to do so for the rest of their professional lives, on either a full-time or hybrid basis.

## What *The Remote Worker's Handbook* Offers

If you want to start working remotely right away, or if you've already had a taste of what it's like, but for whatever reason, things didn't work out, this book will help you succeed as a productive remote worker and truly enjoy the experience.

Each chapter of the *The Remote Worker's Handbook* covers a different aspect of how to achieve success, productivity, and happiness working outside a traditional office. In the past few years, the business world has changed a lot, and this evolution will continue. As a result, even if you opt not to work remotely yourself, you'll likely have to work with others who are, so understanding how the process works is essential.

Failing to become proficient in the latest technologies and tools for communication, collaboration, and online security, for example, will leave you at a professional disadvantage and could put your job security in jeopardy or make you a less desirable candidate for any future jobs you apply for.

To make one thing clear from the start, becoming a remote worker can allow you to live a happier, prosperous, and more well-balanced life, but you will need to learn new skills, adapt to change, and get to know your own wants, needs, and work habits a little better. Will it be easy? Probably not at first. But in time, it'll become second nature.

It's also important to understand that as a remote worker, you may work from your home, a shared work space, or a wide range of locations as you travel. While your work responsibilities will remain the same, the equipment you'll use and your work habits will probably vary depending on where you're working.

To address this, Chapter 4, "How to Set Up and Organize Your Home or Remote Office," focuses on the equipment, tools, and applications you'll need anytime you're working outside a traditional office space. As you'll discover, simply having the right tools and equipment at your disposal is important—but so is a work space that allows you to be productive and to communicate and collaborate effectively.

Becoming a remote worker can provide you with greater freedom and autonomy than you ever thought possible while working for a company, or even when running your own business. We'll begin our exploration into the remote working frontier with an overview of the pros and cons related to becoming a remote worker. That's the focus of Chapter 1, "Pros and Cons of Becoming a Remote Worker," so let's get started!

# Pros and Cons of Becoming a Remote Worker

eople become remote workers for a variety of reasons. Perhaps you're about to begin working from home as an employee of an existing business. Maybe you're self-employed and will operate your own business from home. Whatever the case, if you're accustomed to working from a traditional office, anticipate a rather significant adjustment period, during which you'll need to master a wide range of new skills while adopting new work habits.

Ultimately, you'll need to learn how to communicate and work effectively while staying focused and motivated—

whether you'll be working from home or from a remote work space. The adjustments you'll need to make will largely depend on the type of work you do and your personal work habits. However, for many people, once this adjustment period is over and they've mastered the new skill set required for being a productive remote worker, the benefits of working remotely by far outweigh the drawbacks.

As you'll soon discover, one key to success is having the right equipment on hand and creating a comfortable and distraction-free work space. You'll also need to come up with a way to juggle your personal, family, and job responsibilities while meeting your deadlines, maintaining communication with your employer and team, and effectively managing your time.

Working remotely is not for everyone, although people from all walks of life, holding many job titles, and working in a wide range of industries have found it to be a welcome improvement to their lifestyle from a financial, psychological, and overall job satisfaction standpoint.

Unless you're being forced to work remotely (due to COVID-19 or changes in your company's operations), before you opt to become a part-time or full-time remote worker, determine if it is right for you by considering the pros and cons. Focus on your mindset, desires, skill set, job responsibilities, career goals, and work habits to see if it's a good fit.

## The 16 Biggest Benefits of Working Remotely

There are many pros and cons related to working remotely. This chapter focuses on the most common things people really love about it, as well as what some people don't like about it. By understanding what to expect early on, you'll develop realistic expectations about the challenges and changes you can anticipate in your home and professional life. Let's start by looking at the most common benefits people experience when they begin working remotely.

### 1. No Commute

One of the biggest complaints people often have about working in a traditional office, especially if that office is in or near a city, is the commute. Not only does commuting eat up valuable time from your day, but it also costs money. And when you need to deal with bad traffic or poor weather, it can easily increase stress and anxiety. If you drive to and from work, this also causes wear and tear on your car and requires you to pay for gas, tolls, parking, and more frequent repairs and maintenance.

Carpooling with other people may reduce wear and tear on your vehicle and help protect the environment, but it also means having to coordinate schedules and eliminates any alone time you might enjoy during your commute.

Using mass transit eliminates the need to drive yourself, but besides having to pay for a monthly commuter pass (often out of pocket), you need to get to and from the bus, train, or subway station and then work around the mass transit schedule.

By eliminating their daily commute, remote workers often gain at least one or two extra productive hours in their day. As you'll discover shortly, some people use this time to focus more on themselves and their family. For example, by using your former commuting time to exercise, meditate, get more sleep, pamper yourself, or just take part in activities you truly enjoy, you could improve your overall happiness and stress level.

## 2. Minimal Supervision and More Independence

As a remote worker for an employer, you'll still have a supervisor, manager, or boss to answer to. However, this person will not be constantly looking over your shoulder or micromanaging your day-to-day activities, like they can in a traditional office setting. You'll still be expected to handle all your work responsibilities and meet your deadlines, but it will now be entirely up to you to stay focused, set your schedule, and communicate or collaborate with others using the remote working tools at your disposal.

This is one area where some people especially have problems adapting, because to be a successful remote worker, you need to be a self-starter, have excellent time management skills, and stay organized. Many of the smaller tasks you might once have been able to delegate to someone else may now become your responsibility as well. You'll also need to learn how to avoid common remote-working distractions that could negatively impact your productivity.

On the positive side, by improving your independent thinking, time management, and problem solving, you'll become a more valuable employee. And if you learn how to accomplish all your work responsibilities more efficiently, you could enjoy even more free time in your daily life.

### 3. More Flexible Schedule

Depending on what you do, once you begin working remotely, being "on the job" during preset hours may become less important. And because you can stay in contact with your boss, team, and clients through tools on your smartphone or tablet, you'll likely find you will no longer be chained to your desk.

Yes, you'll still have the same responsibilities—not to mention some additional responsibilities that relate specifically to remote workers—but generally speaking you will have greater control over and more flexibility in your daily work schedule. So by implementing enhanced time management and organizational skills, you'll get more work done in less time, take more breaks throughout your day, or finish a bit earlier in the day than you could when you worked from the company's office.

### 4. Less Office Politics

Whether it's a co-worker who spreads gossip, tries to sabotage your work, takes credit for your accomplishments, or is always either giving advice or criticizing you, there are always people in a traditional office environment you would prefer to avoid altogether. There are often also rules, protocols, and etiquette guidelines that may or may not make sense, but that you must adhere to within an office setting.

While office politics are a very real pitfall of working from a traditional office, when you're working remotely, you're not surrounded by these annoying people and typically are bound by far fewer rules. Sure, you may still need to interact with difficult co-workers via virtual meetings, video calls, emails, and text messages, but the distance makes this much easier. And because all communication is archived, it's much easier for someone to get into trouble for saying or doing something offensive or unacceptable.

## 5. No Dress Code

Depending on the type of work you do and how much interaction you'll have throughout your day with co-workers and clients via video calls and virtual meetings, working from home in your pajamas is rarely possible—nor is it the best approach from a psychological standpoint. To be productive as a working professional, you're better off dressing the part. Formal business attire is certainly not needed, but dressing in casual business attire that's comfortable but looks good is an excellent strategy. While you *can* work in your pajamas, you may find it harder to stay focused on your work, and if your boss or an important client requests an impromptu video call, it's best to be prepared and look professional—not like you just rolled out of bed.

However, working remotely does allow you to dress much more casually and comfortably. Not only can this reduce your clothing budget and dry-cleaning bills, but it will also allow you to dress in a way that better fits your taste and personality.

## 6. Significant Financial Savings

Besides saving money on your commute and wardrobe, when you work remotely, you can often save on food, coffee, and snack expenses, because you do not need to go out to eat for lunch every day and can save a fortune by not spending upward of $6 for each cup of coffee at Starbucks. With a Keurig machine, for example, you can still enjoy gourmet coffee at a fraction of the cost of visiting your favorite coffee shop.

Also, by working from home, you'll be able to spend more time with your kids (and pets) and supervise them, so paying for things like after-school programs, activities, and dog walkers could be less necessary.

According to job search platform Zippia, the average remote worker saves approximately $4,600 per year by not having to commute to work, dress in formal business attire every day, and regularly go out to buy lunch and coffee.

## 7. Fewer In-Person Distractions from Co-Workers

When you're surrounded by co-workers in a traditional office environment, it's all too common for people to constantly socialize, ask questions, solicit advice, interrupt phone calls, or request impromptu meetings about insignificant topics. These interruptions and distractions are reduced when you work remotely, because most meetings are prescheduled and other interactions are handled through messaging, email, or video calls. You can decide when to respond to these messages and calls, so it's much more difficult for others to disrupt your workflow and focus.

## 8. Potentially Better Work-Life Balance

By eliminating your commute and developing better time management skills, you should be able to free up time in your day, determine your own work hours, and better separate your work life and personal life. However, achieving a proper work-life balance is entirely up to you, and it will take discipline. By working from home, for example, you'll be able to see your kids off to school and greet them when they get home. In other words, you have more opportunities to be active in the lives of your kids, yet still hold down a full-time job.

When you work remotely, it's your responsibility to make yourself log off your computer at the end of the workday, so you can focus on your family and personal responsibilities. But on the other hand, during your workday, you can spend time with your kids and pets during breaks and use the time you would otherwise spend commuting to focus more on yourself and your loved ones. Since your home is now potentially your office, you may start to feel obligated to constantly check your incoming emails and voice messages after business hours, respond to Slack messages during dinner, or participate in a work-related business call when you're off the clock and supposed to be watching your child's baseball game or dance recital. When and when not to respond to work-related situations, especially during nights, weekends, and holidays, is part of what it means to develop a clear work-life balance.

## 9. Positive Environmental Impact

Not having to commute to and from work means you're using less gas, creating less pollution, and not contributing to traffic problems. This doesn't just have a positive psychological effect on your life—it also makes a positive impact on the environment.

## 10. Fully Customize Your Work Space

As a remote worker, you can fully personalize and customize your work space by choosing where you work, how you decorate that space, and what equipment you use. Being able to set the temperature in your home office and adjust the lighting will also help ensure your comfort.

Something as simple as choosing the ideal office chair and desk for your work space can have a tremendous impact on your everyday comfort and productivity.

## 11. Develop Better Communication, Time Management, and Organizational Skills

Out of sheer necessity, working remotely will require you to fine-tune your verbal and written communication skills. After all, while in-person communication may become less essential in your daily routine, you will rely heavily on phone calls, video calls, virtual meetings, text messaging, and email, as well as the cloud-based collaboration tools built into many of the applications you'll be using.

Because your schedule will be much more flexible and nobody will pay too much attention to when you're sitting at your desk, it will be your responsibility to manage your time efficiently. You'll be expected to juggle a broader range of tasks while still meeting your deadlines. Thus, you must be able to avoid common distractions, overcome technical snafus, and complete your work in a timely manner.

Working remotely will also require superior organizational skills, since you'll likely need to manage your own meeting schedule, keep track of more digital files, and complete tasks that were once handled by an office support staff—without allowing anything to fall through the cracks.

Learning these skills is relatively easy. Mastering them is a bit more challenging, because you may need to alter your workflow and change your work habits while getting used to a new collection of applications. If you dedicate yourself to adopting these new skills, they'll become second nature in no time, and they'll make you a more valuable employee—or a more efficient business operator.

## 12. Tax Incentives

The federal government (and perhaps your state) offers a nice selection of tax incentives to remote workers (particularly those who are self-employed or work freelance), including deductions for operating a homebased office and having to purchase your own equipment.

You'll even be able to write off at least a portion of your home's utility bills, mortgage interest/rent, real estate taxes (if applicable), various insurance fees, internet fees, and other work expenses. Unfortunately, the tax deductions are not as generous for remote workers who are not self-employed.

You'll want to speak with an accountant once you begin working remotely to determine exactly what types of tax incentives and deductions you're entitled to. To learn more, visit bit.ly/3rRkmPu.

Make sure to keep meticulous financial records and copies of receipts if you plan to take advantage of the tax deductions associated with working from home. Some people find it easier from a record keeping standpoint to open a separate bank account or use a separate credit card exclusively to cover their home office and work expenses.

## 13. Increased Job Satisfaction

Whether it results from a more independent and flexible schedule, being able to achieve a better work-life balance, or the money you'll save by not having to commute and eat out for lunch, there are many reasons 97 percent of people questioned for a 2022 study conducted by Buffer say that they'd choose to work remotely for the rest of their career, even if it were just on a part-time basis.

By eliminating many of the minor (and sometimes major) frustrations of working from a traditional office, many people find their jobs to be even more rewarding and emotionally fulfilling.

## 14. Fewer Absences from Work

There's something to be said about being able to roll out of bed and start work from your home office in a matter of minutes when necessary. By not surrounding yourself with other people during your workday, your chances of being exposed to germs and getting sick drop dramatically. However, if you do catch a cold, you'll likely still be able to work from home and be productive. This will reduce your number of sick days and full-day absences from work each year.

### 15. More Time with Kids and Pets

Whether it's before school or after they get home, as a remote worker with a more flexible schedule, you'll likely have additional time to spend with your kids. You'll also be able to take your dog on walks throughout the day, better bond with your pet, alleviate their separation anxiety, and potentially save hundreds of dollars per month by not having to hire a dog walker.

### 16. Potentially More Personal Time

One scheduling strategy some remote workers implement is to use the time they previously spent commuting as personal time. How you define that is up to you. You can take time to enjoy a hobby, spend time with a pet or family members, meditate, listen to music, catch up on the latest news, converse with friends, read a book, or focus on some type of personal growth or enrichment activity.

## The 14 Biggest Drawbacks of Working Remotely

Being a remote worker certainly has its advantages. There are, however, also some potential pitfalls. The good news is that if you understand and can identify these drawbacks and how they might affect you, it's very easy to eliminate or diminish the negative impact each can have. Let's look at some of the most common complaints people have about remote working. As you go through this list, try to determine which might apply to your situation. Then consider all your options for addressing the issue—always with the goal of ensuring your happiness and productivity.

### 1. Finding a Comfortable and Conducive Work Location

Working from home is only one option for remote work. Some remote workers wind up in a shared work space that is not affiliated with their employer. For people who are constantly on the go, their most frequent work space might be a coffee shop, hotel room, airplane, airport, or public library.

If you will be working from home, it's essential to create a work space that's conducive to your work habits and workflow. It needs to be comfortable, spacious, well-lit, and maintain a proper temperature, while giving you easy access to all the tools and equipment you need. Chapter 4, "How to Set Up and Organize Your Home or Remote Office," covers everything you need to consider when choosing where to work and the equipment you'll need to get your work done.

As you'll discover, problems with your work space will affect your productivity, attitude, and physical comfort. Even what seems like a minor inconvenience at first could lead to a larger issue if not properly dealt with.

## 10 THINGS TO CONSIDER WHEN CHOOSING YOUR WORK SPACE

Let's look at 10 things to consider when deciding on your work space. We'll explore the true impact of each of these considerations a bit later. Right now, just start thinking about where you plan to work from, what you'll need to enhance your work space, and what potential problems you might encounter in your selected location.

1. *Accessibility to tools and equipment you need.* If, due to space limitations, your desk is in one part of the room but your printer is on the opposite side of the room, this will be a hassle every time you need to get up from your desk to retrieve a printout. Consider all the equipment and devices you'll need to keep plugged into an electrical outlet and how close your desk is to that power source. Ideally, you want to avoid extension cords, power strips, and other cables stretching across open areas of your floor or getting tangled behind your desk.

2. *Décor.* Whether it's the color of the walls, photographs, artwork, houseplants, or other décor, the things you look at day after day will have a psychological impact on you. If you don't like the way your work space looks, this can affect your mood and productivity level.

## 10 THINGS TO CONSIDER, CONT.

3. *Ergonomic design, height, and comfort of your desk chair*. You'll be sitting in the same office chair every day, for between eight and ten hours per day. It needs to be comfortable, be able to adjust to the perfect height for your desk, and provide support to your lower back and arms. If the chair does not properly fit your body type or can't be adjusted properly, in the short term you'll be uncomfortable, but over a period of months or years you could develop problems with your back, neck, shoulders, arms, and wrists. If you spend money on only one thing in your work space, make it your chair. If you're working outside your home, choose a location with a comfortable place to sit. If the seating situation isn't ideal, be sure to stand up, stretch, and take short walks often throughout your day to minimize the negative physical impact on you.

4. *Height and size of the desk*. In addition to the size, adjustability, and comfort of your desk chair, you also need to choose a proper desk and work area. Whether it's a traditional desk, your dining room table, a folding table, or a small table at a coffee shop, your work area needs to be the proper height and provide enough space for you to work comfortably. If your work area is small (such as when you're a frequent air traveler in coach class), the size of your laptop will become an important consideration.

5. *Lighting*. If your work area is too dimly lit, it will cause eyestrain. If it's too bright, it might wind up causing headaches. Similarly, if you're surrounded by the wrong type of lighting for extended periods or the position of the primary light source is not correct, this can also cause fatigue, headaches, and other eye issues. For example, fluorescent lighting in your home office is the worst option.

6. *Noise level*. Some people can concentrate with crowds of people around, the TV or music playing in the background, or other noisy distractions. Plenty of people, however, are bothered by too much noise. Consider the ambient noise level where you plan to work. How will it affect you? Will the noise impact your phone calls and virtual meetings? What can be done to control or eliminate the noise? Could you wear headphones with a noise-cancelation feature in order to concentrate?

## 10 THINGS TO CONSIDER, CONT.

7. *Number of distractions.* When working outside a traditional office, you'll encounter many distractions from other people, pets, ambient noises, and other causes you might not be able to control. First, identify what these distractions might be in your chosen work space, and then determine what you'll need to do to reduce or eliminate them. Having a door you can close, setting ground rules for when other people can enter your work space, or installing inexpensive sound dampeners on the walls might be viable solutions for reducing distractions.

8. *Proximity to power and internet.* Most remote workers rely on equipment, such as their computer, that needs a power source and continuous access to a strong internet connection. If your chosen work space lacks an ample number of electrical outlets or the wifi signal is too weak, it can affect your productivity level. It might make sense to have additional outlets installed in your home office, move your modem closer, or add wifi signal boosters to your home. If you'll be working outside your home, you'll likely want to carry a power strip with you and make sure your smartphone can generate a personal wifi hotspot to ensure internet connectivity.

9. *Temperature.* If you're too hot or too cold or the air quality is too dry, too humid, or has a bad smell, this will impact your ability to focus and be comfortable while you're working. When working from a basement, garage, or attic, pay extra attention to air quality, especially issues relating to mold and mildew.

10. *Size of the space.* Forcing yourself to work from an area that's too small will be uncomfortable and frustrating. Again, a lot has to do with your personal work habits and where you're working from, so pay attention to your space needs and be sure to cater to them—especially if you'll be working from that location for more than a few hours at a time. For example, if you traditionally place paperwork next to your laptop while you're working, the table or desk you choose needs to accommodate this.

## 2. Sharing Your Work Space with Others

During the shelter-at-home period of the COVID-19 pandemic, many people were forced to share a work space with a spouse, a roommate, and/or children. They had to fight for desk space and internet bandwidth and struggle to focus amid the constant distractions.

Even if you're extremely social, it's important to evaluate your work habits and determine if you do better surrounded by other people or if you're more productive having a work space to yourself.

Some people find that working from home, when they can be alone during their workday, is ideal. Others find it disconcerting. If you're one of the latter, a shared work space or a coffee shop may be a more congenial atmosphere for you.

## 3. Not Having Access to an In-Person Secretary or Assistant

Being a remote worker often means that you're responsible for all the tasks that a secretary, office assistant, or personal assistant might have done for you in the past, such as managing your schedule, taking dictation, photocopying, filing, screening calls, or making coffee. You'll need to learn how to handle these and other tasks on your own so that you can maintain the same level of efficiency.

If you do have a support staff, but they too are working remotely from another location, you'll still need to adapt your work habits and perhaps learn how to use a new set of communication and collaboration tools.

## 4. Avoiding Personal and Family-Related Distractions During the Workday

Unless you live alone and don't have any pets or overly friendly neighbors, working from home will probably mean you'll encounter personal distractions during your workday. In this situation, setting ground rules with the people you live with is essential. But having a work space with a door you can close will also be beneficial. As a remote worker, you'll likely have more time to spend with the people you care about. However, you will need to learn how to better manage your schedule and juggle your personal and professional responsibilities.

## 5. Dealing with Isolation and Lack of Socialization

Perhaps the biggest complaint remote workers have is dealing with the isolation and the lack of socialization with their co-workers. There's a huge difference between having in-person meetings or gathering around the water cooler at the office to gossip and talking to those same people on the phone and during virtual meetings.

Chapter 10, "The Psychological Aspect of Working Remotely," focuses on how to deal with feelings of loneliness, isolation, and lack of socialization with your colleagues and superiors. Occasionally feeling isolated while working remotely is normal, and there are a wide range of strategies and activities you can implement to reduce or eliminate these feelings—especially when you're not being forced into seclusion by a pandemic.

## 6. Staying Motivated and Focused

No matter what you do for work and what responsibilities you're forced to juggle, there will be times when staying motivated and focused on what you need to accomplish will be challenging. It can become even more difficult if there's nobody around to motivate you in person. We'll focus on some strategies for staying motivated and focused later, but right now, understand this can become a challenge if you're new to remote working, but you're accustomed to being part of a culture within your organization that previously involved a lot of in-person interaction with your co-workers or team.

## 7. Acquiring the Necessary Equipment

You will need a collection of tools, equipment, applications, and resources to meet your professional responsibilities while working remotely. Some employers provide everything you require, but sometimes it will be your job not just to identify what you need, but also to pay out-of-pocket to acquire it. Chapter 4, "How to Set Up and Organize Your Home or Remote Office," will help you figure out what you need and offer money-saving options for purchasing the ideal collection of tools and equipment.

If you're responsible for buying everything you'll need to be a successful remote worker, be sure to focus on compatibility with your employer and co-workers to ensure seamless integration. If you're using a Mac with

Apple Pages for word processing, but your co-workers are using Microsoft Word on Windows PCs or Google Docs, you could encounter file compatibility issues when exchanging documents or trying to collaborate in real time online. Ideally, your employer will provide specific guidelines for what equipment and tools to use, but if not, you'll need to coordinate carefully with the people you work with.

### 8. Needing to Learn New Communication and Collaboration Skills

Because of the newfound popularity of remote working (and the COVID-19 pandemic), a vast new selection of communication and collaboration tools is now available. Whether it's for participating in video calls and virtual meetings, exchanging text messages, remotely (and securely) sharing data and files via the cloud, communicating via email, or collaborating in real time, once your company or team chooses what tools you'll be using, it's essential to quickly become competent using them. Having technical issues with your computer's camera or microphone when you're supposed to be in a virtual meeting is not acceptable; neither is double-booking your time for taking part in calls or virtual meetings.

You and your team should set ground rules for what is and is not acceptable during virtual interactions; of course, anything that would be inappropriate in a traditional workplace setting continues to be inappropriate in a virtual setting. Also make it clear whether everyone is expected to turn on their cameras and when it's appropriate to ask a question or unmute their microphone to speak up. If you're not sure what's accepted etiquette for your team, contact your superior and ask for clarification.

For emails, text messaging, and real-time collaboration with co-workers, determine whether your company's culture finds emojis or abbreviations acceptable. Likewise, make sure you can communicate clearly (in writing and verbally); when you're using remote working tools, the chances of a misunderstanding become much greater. Something as simple as using incorrect punctuation, a typo, or the wrong word could affect how your message is interpreted by the recipient.

Using too many abbreviations does not always make you sound more intelligent. In fact, it can become very confusing, so it's often a good idea to spell everything out.

Also, a simple observation can easily be misconstrued as a criticism or insult. Get into the habit of thinking before you speak and proofreading all your texts and emails before you send them. This is also important if you have autocorrect turned on in whatever communication tool you're using.

Because software tools are continuously being updated with new features and functions, it's your responsibility not just to learn how to use them, but also to stay up-to-date when things change. The easiest way to do this is to rely on free tutorials and how-to videos from the companies that developed the tools.

If your company relies on Slack as a communications tool, go to the Slack website (slack.com/), click on the Resources menu option, and then visit the Slack Help Center. Here you'll find free articles, how-to videos, and other content to help you learn about the features and functions of this tool. If you have a question about how to use a specific feature, you could ask a co-worker or visit YouTube (youtube.com/). Within the YouTube Search field, enter your question, and then watch a free video that provides the answer or advice you need.

Chapter 6, "How to Remotely Collaborate," provides information about the most common tools used by remote workers. As you learn about what each of these tools is used for, you'll also be provided with resources for becoming proficient using them in the quickest and most inexpensive way possible.

## 9. Dealing with Security-Related Issues

Your work probably requires you to deal with data, documents, files, and information that is private or that needs to be kept secure. When you're working remotely and relying on the internet, this opens you and your employer up to a wide range of security issues and the greater chance of a data breach.

As you'll discover from Chapter 8, "Effectively Deal with Online Security and Privacy Issues," there are several simple things you can do to ensure your own privacy and security when working online, while protecting information and data owned by your employer. What you need to understand for online security is that most issues happen because of human error. Someone clicks on the wrong thing, shares a file with the wrong person, accidentally tells the wrong person their account password, gets caught in a social engineering or phishing scheme, or accidentally downloads a virus or malware onto their computer or mobile device.

Besides exercising common sense for online security, you'll want to install the right security tools onto your computer, smartphone, and tablet. Hopefully, your employer will dictate which tools to use and supply them, but at the very least, you want to be using a Virtual Private Network (VPN) when working from any wifi hotspot, install virus protection software onto your computer, plus turn on two-factor authentication for all the online applications and tools that offer it. You also want to get into the habit of using a separate, secure password for each of your accounts, and then periodically changing those passwords.

You'll learn more about what the best security tools are, how to use them, and what they cost in Chapter 8. Right now, all you need to know is that you do not need to become a computer engineer to help ensure your online security and protect your employer's data. You do, however, need to make certain you're using the best possible tools and taking the proper precautions. Fortunately, that's relatively simple to do.

### 10. Not Balancing Your Work and Personal Life

When your office is part of your home or your remote working equipment can come with you wherever you go, it can be very difficult to separate your personal and professional life. If you get a work email or text message while you're watching your child's evening soccer game or during family dinner, you may be inclined to respond immediately from your smartphone or tablet.

As a remote worker, you must learn how to shut down once your workday ends. You also need to determine if an after-hours message is a real emergency that needs to be dealt with immediately, or if it can wait until the next business day. Of course, you want to be an attentive and responsible worker, but you also need to maintain your personal life. Depending on what you do for a living, your expected work hours, and your relationship with your employer, you must set boundaries and define your work hours in a way that addresses your employer's needs while giving you the freedom to enjoy a personal life.

Expect some challenges while learning to achieve a healthy balance between your personal and professional life. Some concessions may need to be made, and sometimes flexibility is important. However, your employer should not expect you to be accessible and responsive on a 24/7 basis.

## 11. Paying for Home Office Expenses

Depending on your employer, the expenses you incur as a remote worker may become your responsibility. You may need to pay out of pocket for your internet service, smartphone and cellular bill, printer paper and ink (toner), and personal subscriptions to certain cloud-based services or security tools. You may also need to purchase and maintain your own computer(s), home office furniture, and whatever other equipment you'll need for your job.

So while you may save money on your daily commute, new types of expenses will probably arise. Talk to your employer about exactly what they will cover and what you're responsible for, and then speak with your own accountant to determine what expenses (if any) should be deducted on your income taxes.

## 12. Less In-Person Time with Your Employer

One potential problem of working remotely is that you wind up spending a lot less face-to-face time with your boss. You will have to work to ensure that they understand the work you're doing, your value to the company, and your accomplishments. How you achieve this will vary. For instance, you could set up a weekly, monthly, or annual meeting to discuss your goals, responsibilities, and accomplishments. It might also be useful to give your supervisor full access to your schedule or maintain a shared document that lists your objectives and responsibilities for each day, week, or month.

Once you begin working remotely, it becomes more important for everyone on your team (especially you and your superior) to clearly understand your job description and your responsibilities, and for you to understand exactly what your employer expects of you. This should all be clearly addressed in writing so there is less chance of misunderstandings.

## 13. Lack of Relationship with Co-Workers

Unless you're able to meet up with your co-workers in person for social gatherings, it is difficult to develop or maintain friendships with them as a remote worker. When you take part in a video call or virtual meeting, there will typically be an agenda in place, as well as a scheduled duration for the interaction, so you won't have time to chitchat. You could go months without realizing a co-worker is pregnant, until one day they disappear for their maternity leave.

Meanwhile, unless you develop a way to have personal conversations, you'll miss out on discussing the trials and tribulations in the lives of your co-workers. That may sound like a benefit, but it also makes it difficult to get to know them. Most times you'll wind up needing to seek your social outlets elsewhere or try to meet up with them outside of office hours. When co-workers are in different cities, this becomes even more of a challenge.

If your goal is to establish and maintain friendships with your superiors and co-workers, you'll want to set up times to chat informally or meet up in person for a meal, coffee, or drinks. Also remember to acknowledge your co-workers' birthdays, work anniversaries, and accomplishments.

When possible, set up a virtual place where you can exchange personal messages and engage in conversations outside of work (while maintaining proper office etiquette). Keep in mind that if you use a company-provided communications tool, transcripts of your discussions are archived and your superiors will have access to them.

To maintain some level of socialization with your team, consider setting up virtual (or in person) social gatherings and team-building activities once or twice per month. Encourage people to share information about themselves and their lives outside of work, and if you notice someone is facing a personal or professional challenge, ask them if they need help.

## 14. More Virtual Meetings

Because you won't be face-to-face with your co-workers and superiors (or perhaps even your clients, if applicable), you'll likely need to take part in more video calls and virtual meetings. You may also discover that workplace etiquette is to preschedule calls and meetings, so in addition to setting aside time in your day for calls and meetings (and to get camera-ready), you'll need to invest more time in managing your schedule.

On the plus side, you can take part in video calls using your smartphone, tablet, or laptop, so you don't have to be stuck at your desk all day. And because many of the video calling and virtual meeting applications allow you to use virtual backgrounds, the people you're meeting with don't need to know where you are when you're speaking with them.

## The Pros and Cons of Working from a Shared Work Space

Remote workers who prefer not to work at home can instead pay a daily, weekly, or monthly fee to use a shared work space that's not associated with their employer. This is typically a facility that offers a collection of desks, small offices (or meeting rooms), and tools needed for a group of people to work in a communal area.

A shared work space is an added expense, but it can help remote workers overcome the loneliness and isolation sometimes associated with working from home. It also provides a space that's pre-equipped with the tools you might need, like high-speed public wifi, a comfortable desk and chair, a shared printer, and plenty of coffee and snacks.

Remember that because this is a shared work space, people can often overhear your phone conversations or video calls, so privacy is a consideration. There's also the ongoing challenge of dealing with interruptions from others (who are office mates in the shared work space, but not co-workers from your company). Like every other remote work option, a shared work space has its pros and cons. When you visit some of these locations in your area, you'll likely find that their amenities and work atmospheres vary, as do their fees.

To find a shared work space close to you, launch your favorite internet search engine and type "shared work space" in the search field. There are a handful of national chains as well as many independent and locally owned operations. Some of the national chains include:

⋯▶ *Regus*: regus.com/en-us/office-space
⋯▶ *Spaces*: spacesworks.com/

⋅▹ *Staples Studio*: staples.com/sbd/cre/noheader/staples_studio/
⋅▹ *WeWork*: wework.com/

Chapter 5, "Work Successfully from a Shared Work Space," focuses specifically on how to choose and be productive in this type of remote work environment. A free option is simply to pack up your laptop, smartphone, and related gear and work from a nearby coffee shop. The atmosphere is loud and busy (because of the steady flow of customers), but some people prefer this to working from home or a hotel room.

## Determine If You're Cut Out to Work Remotely

Now that you've learned about some of the pros and cons of being a remote worker, use the questionnaire in Figure 1.1 below to help you determine if this type of work situation is suitable for you.

FIGURE 1.1—**Remote Worker Questionnaire**

What are your top five reasons for wanting to become a remote worker?

1. _____

2. _____

3. _____

4. _____

5. _____

What equipment and tools would you need to purchase immediately to successfully work outside a traditional office?

_____

_____

_____

_____

FIGURE 1.1—**Remote Worker Questionnaire,** cont.

As a remote worker, where do you expect to be working from and how conducive is this space for working? How will you need to alter the space to make it more useful?

_____

_____

_____

_____

Based on your unique situation, what are the top five biggest distractions you expect will need to be overcome daily as a remote worker?

1. _____

2. _____

3. _____

4. _____

5. _____

Once you're working remotely, how do you expect your life will change?

_____

_____

_____

_____

By not having to commute to and from work each day, how would you like to spend that additional time? What personal enrichment, fitness, or wellness activities might you engage in?

_____

_____

_____

_____

FIGURE 1.1—**Remote Worker Questionnaire,** cont.

Based on your situation, how might working remotely impact your personal work-life balance?

_____

_____

_____

_____

Based on your work habits and personality, what do you expect will be the three biggest challenges or drawbacks to becoming a remote worker?

1. _____

2. _____

3. _____

What skills do you think you'll need to acquire or improve on to become successful and productive as a remote worker? What additional applications or tools will you need to become proficient in using?

_____

_____

_____

_____

Based on the money you'll potentially save, and the additional expenses you may become responsible for, how do you expect remote working will impact your personal or family finances?

_____

_____

_____

FIGURE 1.1—**Remote Worker Questionnaire,** cont.

What are your three biggest fears about working remotely?

1. _____

2. _____

3. _____

How do you expect your working relationship with your superiors and co-workers will change once you begin working remotely? How will you compensate for these changes?

_____

_____

_____

_____

## Becoming a Remote Worker Will Require Developing a New Skill Set

As you continue reading this book, refer back to the answers you provided when completing the above questionnaire. Based on your current mindset, expectations, and goals, the answers you provided will help you achieve success faster as you learn what's possible when working remotely.

Besides adapting to a new work schedule, many remote workers need to develop or improve on certain skills to succeed. Verbal and written communication skills will become more essential than ever. With minimal in-person interaction, you'll now primarily be communicating via phone calls, video calls, virtual meetings, email, text and instant messaging (IMs), and online collaboration tools.

If you're not satisfied with the level of your written communication skills, there are tools available—like advanced spelling and grammar checkers—that can help. ProWritingAid (prowritingaid.com), for one, is a grammar checker, style editor, and writing mentor available on a subscription basis. It works with popular word processors, web browsers, email clients, and other applications you'll use when writing.

Learning new skills and how to adapt to a change in your daily workflow is the focus of Chapter 2, "Being a Successful Remote Worker Is a Skill Set unto Itself." Learning these skills is generally not difficult, but it will take some time to become proficient using them.

# Being a Successful Remote Worker Is a Skill Set unto Itself

Becoming a remote worker means taking on a lot of independence and decision-making power (at least for yourself). Of course, if you have a supervisor, team leader, or boss, you still must answer to them and adhere to your employer's guidelines and demands. However, during your workday, you'll typically have a lot more autonomy.

In addition to the skill set that's required to do your job, to succeed working remotely, you'll need to become highly proficient in four skill areas:

1. Written communication
2. Verbal communication
3. Time management
4. Collaborating using cloud-based tools

This chapter examines why these skills are essential and how to get the training you'll need to incorporate them into your workflow. At the same time, you'll need to develop the required mentality to keep you focused and motivated. From a psychological standpoint, you want to avoid falling victim to feelings of isolation or loneliness. We will also touch on preparing yourself mentally to become an efficient remote worker and explain how to avoid some of the most common pitfalls that first-time remote workers face.

## Develop Your Written Communication Skills

As a remote worker, you'll likely need to forgo many of the in-person and face-to-face interactions you'd otherwise have with your co-workers, team members, superiors, customers, and clients. Often, you'll communicate via email, text messaging, file sharing, and online collaboration tools.

For this reason, enhancing your written communication skills is extremely important. It's far too easy to make errors when writing that can either make you seem unintelligent or lead to misunderstandings. Something as simple as a grammatical error or using the wrong word can change the meaning or intent of what you're trying to say.

All sorts of business writing classes are available online that will help improve your written communication skills over time. However, to achieve immediate results, begin using the spelling and grammar checker that's built into your word processor. You should also take advantage of apps that check your spelling, grammar, and overall writing style across all the applications you commonly use, including email, messaging, collaboration tools, and word processing.

Two options are subscription-based: Grammarly (grammarly.com/) and ProWritingAid (prowritingaid.com). Either can be set up to work in real time as you're writing or to review your work after you're done (but before you share it with others). In addition to serving as a spelling and grammar checker, these tools work as a style editor and writing mentor. So along with fixing basic mistakes, over time they're designed to teach you key skills that'll make you a better writer.

ProWritingAid, for example, can be used as a stand-alone, online tool. However, once you subscribe to the service, you can download and install plug-ins that work directly with popular email clients (like Microsoft Outlook), word processors (like Microsoft Word, Google Docs, and OpenOffice), and commonly used web browsers (including Microsoft Edge, Google Chrome, Apple Safari, and Firefox).

To help determine if your business writing skills need polishing, The Business Writing Center website offers a selection of free writing proficiency tests. You can take them at bit.ly/3VpIgiD.

Keep in mind, business writing is different from technical, marketing, or sales-oriented writing, which may or may not be relevant to your work. The following are examples of online business writing courses you can participate in if you're willing to invest the time. Most of these classes will require between 10 and 20 hours to complete.

- *Business Writing (Coursera)*: bit.ly/3EFKvZ1
- *The Business Writing Center* (offers seven different courses): bit.ly/3SXu2Us
- *Business Writing for Results* (Pryor Learning): bit.ly/3g5tBch
- *Business Writing Principles* (LinkedIn Learning): bit.ly/3S15iJA
- *Effective Business Writing Techniques Course* (Instructional Solutions): bit.ly/3MnV6d3
- *High-Impact Business Writing* (Coursera): bit.ly/3RWMifd
- *Persuasive Communication: Narrative, Evidence, and Impact* (Harvard University): hks.harvard.edu/educational-programs
- *Tips for Better Business Writing* (LinkedIn Learning): bit.ly/3MG3Ew9

You'll also find online classes that focus on business writing specifically for emails, reports, proposals, or text messaging. Some of these more specialized classes can be found on the Udemy online learning platform (udemy.com/topic/business-writing/). Your best strategy is to incorporate a writing tool, like ProWritingAid, into your daily routine. Then as you have time, take a business writing course to further polish your skills.

## Verbal Communication Is Also an Important Skill to Master

Whether you're communicating in person, over the phone, during a video call, or in a virtual meeting, being able to get your point across, be easily understood, and be someone whom people want to listen to is a skill unto itself. Of course, how you conduct yourself when speaking will vary greatly depending on whom you're speaking with and the situation you're in.

Developing a strong vocabulary and honing your speaking skills will make you a more versatile verbal communicator in any situation. However, just knowing the right words to say and when to say them is only part of the equation. Becoming a proficient verbal communicator requires practice, confidence, timing, and poise. You also need to understand your audience—whether it's one person or a group—and adapt your speaking style and approach accordingly.

After all, you'll likely speak with your boss, a client, or a co-worker very differently than you'd speak with your partner, best friend, or child. Equally important is that you thoroughly understand the information you're trying to communicate. This will boost your confidence, enhance your credibility, and make you a better communicator.

## How and Where to Get the Training and Coaching You Might Need

If you have the budget and time, working one-on-one with a communication coach can be very beneficial. This is like working with a vocal coach if you're a singer, but the focus is on using your speaking voice and becoming a better verbal communicator. You can also take online classes you can take that provide the same information, but without a personalized approach or critique.

Public speaking courses are offered by a wide range of colleges and online training services, including:

- *Dale Carnegie*: dalecarnegie.com
- *MasterClass*: masterclass.com
- *Moxie Institute*: moxieinstitute.com
- *Skillshare*: skillshare.com/

## 12 TIPS FOR MORE EFFECTIVE VERBAL COMMUNICATION

Whenever you're speaking in a professional situation, use these tips:

1. *Always think before you speak*. Will what you're about to say offend anyone? Consider your audience and adjust your approach accordingly.

2. *Be confident*. This will help you quickly build credibility with the people you're communicating with. Show that you understand what you're talking about by using appropriate terminology. Your word choice, the tone of your voice, your ability to maintain eye contact, and your body language will all help you project confidence and credibility whenever you speak.

3. *Don't mix up your words or ideas*. Be as clear and concise as possible, using short and easy-to-understand sentences.

4. *Pay attention to the tone of your voice*. Speaking in a monotone isn't just boring to listen to—it makes you less credible. Be sure to inject emotion into your speech pattern, especially when you want to add emphasis to your key points.

5. *Use appropriate body language*. While this is particularly important in person or during a video call or virtual meeting, your facial expressions, gestures, eye contact, and how you engage with others are all part of being a good verbal communicator.

6. *Don't just speak—listen and engage in a conversation*. When asking a question, phrase it as an open-ended question to generate a more detailed and informative response. When listening to someone else speak, don't make rash judgments, ask for clarification when necessary, and focus on what they're saying. Never interrupt. Wait until they're done speaking before you respond.

7. *Use humor when it's appropriate*. But never say or do anything in a work situation that someone could find offensive.

## 12 TIPS, CONT.

8. *Avoid controversial topics.* That includes religion, politics, or discussing your salary with co-workers.

9. *Focus on being yourself.* If your audience feels you're being inauthentic or trying too hard to be someone you're not, it will generate distrust. Present yourself as genuinely as you can and be honest. If you don't know something, admit it. If you make a mistake, apologize and take responsibility.

10. *Don't speak too fast.* Especially if you're nervous, you may wind up speaking too quickly or in a garbled or muffled voice. Take the time to breathe, insert appropriate pauses into what you're saying, and make sure you're enunciating each word clearly. Remember, how you present information is as important as what information you're trying to communicate.

11. *When speaking with one or two other people, use their names.* This will help you build a stronger rapport, maintain their attention, and demonstrate that what you're saying is relevant to the people you're speaking with.

12. *Practice speaking in front of groups.* If you're not comfortable speaking in front of multiple people or presenting yourself on camera during a video call or virtual meeting, practice with someone you trust or in front of a mirror. Remember, preparation and practice will help boost your confidence and abilities.

## Master the Art of Managing Your Time

One problem some remote workers face, especially if they have co-workers in different time zones, is developing a set work schedule. In a typical office setting, you may be expected to work a traditional eight-hour day, between 9 A.M. and 5 P.M., with a lunch hour and several short breaks throughout the day. However, as a remote worker, it's often hard to stick with a regular schedule.

Developing your time management skills will help you to:

→ Complete your work responsibilities within a predetermined number of hours per day or week

## TOASTMASTERS OFFERS LOW-COST TRAINING FOR PUBLIC SPEAKERS

If you have the time and inclination, another way to enhance your verbal communication and public speaking skills is to practice speaking and presenting in front of an audience. One way to do this is to participate in an organization called Toastmasters (toastmasters.org/).

Founded in 1924, Toastmasters is a nonprofit organization with more than 14,000 clubs worldwide. Its goal is to help people in all occupations develop their listening, planning, motivational, and team-building skills. Most important, participating in Toastmasters will help you overcome your fear of public speaking and become a better verbal communicator.

When you join a Toastmasters club, in addition to learning basic public speaking skills, you're encouraged to practice them in front of fellow members, who will then provide constructive evaluations. A typical meeting lasts between one and two hours. However, in addition to the individual weekly or biweekly meetings, their website has a vast collection of learning materials you can use.

The membership fee is $45 every six months. To learn about local Toastmasters meetings in your area, visit toastmasters.org/find-a-club.

- Avoid wasting time on unimportant tasks
- Prioritize what's important and focus on essential tasks
- Delegate tasks when necessary
- Avoid being a slave to your smartphone or computer
- Become more productive and efficient
- Never miss important meetings or deadlines
- Avoid procrastinating, especially when it comes to tasks you don't enjoy
- Better juggle your personal and professional life

Time management is all about learning how to use your time effectively, so that you spend an appropriate amount of time on the most essential activities, without allowing yourself to get bogged down with nonessential busywork.

An effective time manager plans out their day in advance. This means determining the most important tasks that need to get accomplished, prioritizing everything that must get done each day, allocating specific amounts of time for each task, blocking out distractions, allowing some flexibility in your schedule for unexpected events, and scheduling breaks throughout the day to avoid burnout.

The first step in improving your time management skills is to carefully evaluate how you spend every minute of your day and track your schedule in writing for at least one week. This time audit will allow you to identify your biggest time wasters, determine when and why you're procrastinating, and pinpoint when your time is being poorly managed.

During your personal time audit period, use a stopwatch or timer. Write down everything you do, no matter how inconsequential, and document how much time you spend on each task. Some people document their days in 15- or 30-minute increments, or write down everything they do from the moment they wake up in the morning until the time they go to bed.

Once your time audit is complete, determine when and how you become distracted, what unimportant tasks you wound up wasting a lot of time on, what gaps in your schedule could have been put to more productive use, and in what circumstances you were the most productive and the least productive.

While it may seem that learning to multitask will be an efficient way to get more done in less time, it is seldom the best solution. When you multitask, you're pulling your attention away from individual tasks, trying to get multiple things done at the same time, and increasing your chance of making mistakes. Anytime you make a mistake, it could result in wasted money, frustration, increased stress, and the need to invest even more time to fix the problem.

In most situations, you're better off focusing on just one task at a time. Prioritize your work so that you're focusing on your most important tasks during the times of the day when you're most alert and productive. And when you're focused on getting a task done, make a conscious effort to avoid distractions. It's also useful to give yourself a deadline or time limit for each task and always stay focused on the big picture, which is your overall goal or objective.

Without a supervisor or co-workers keeping tabs on what you're doing, it's your responsibility to determine how you spend every minute of your day. It's easy to allow your workday to leak into your personal time or to avoid taking breaks (which ultimately leads to exhaustion). Someone who is good at time management makes sure to schedule 5- to 15-minute breaks throughout their day to relax, clear their mind, take a short walk, and smoothly transition from one task to the next.

## Prioritize Each Task

Especially when you're focused on a task, it's very easy to lose track of time. For this reason, you'll want to take advantage of a proven time management tool you can customize to match your work habits. This might be a calendar/scheduling application on your smartphone, tablet, or computer, or it could be a printed day planner that allows you to divide your day into 15- to 30-minute increments.

Either first thing in the morning or as the last thing you do each work-day, invest at least 15 minutes to plan out the day ahead. Write down all your required meetings and the tasks you must accomplish that day. Give each task a priority, such as:

- *Time-sensitive*: These tasks have a specific deadline and are extremely important. They might include meetings that start and end at a specific time.
- *Essential*: These might include tasks that need to get completed by the end of the day or week, but they have no set time or dead-line.
- *Important*: These are things you need to get done eventually, but they have no deadline or can be pushed back when an unscheduled time-sensitive or essential task comes up.
- *Nonessential*: These are things you need to do but have minimal importance. Add these items to an ongoing to-do list that you can focus on when you have breaks in your schedule. In addition to the

scheduled tasks that appear in your calendar or planner, maintain one or more relevant to-do lists that contain your nonessential tasks.

- ⸱▸ *Delegate*: These are tasks you can assign a co-worker or support staffer to handle.
- ⸱▸ *Unimportant*: This task has little to no relevance to your work responsibilities, and you shouldn't waste any significant time on it.

Within your to-do lists or schedule, these task priorities could be abbreviated or color-coded as "TS" (red), "E" (orange), "I" (green), "NE" (blue), "D" (purple), or "U" (brown). You could also indicate the priority of a task by associating one to three stars with it. Use any system that works for you.

Break down each of your larger tasks into several smaller and more manageable ones, listing them in the order they need to be accomplished, with a deadline or time frame associated with each. Then insert all the smaller tasks into your schedule in a way that'll allow you to complete the overall task by your designated deadline.

Also keep separate lists of tasks that need to get accomplished by the end of the week, the end of the month, or the end of the quarter. Based on the pending deadlines for these tasks and subtasks, determine if you need to work them into your daily schedule.

Once you know what you need to accomplish and what your upcoming priorities are, insert each task into your daily or weekly schedule. When doing this, consider when you're most alert and efficient. Some people are most productive first thing in the morning, while others can focus better at midday or toward the end of their workday. Based on your work habits and preferences, try to schedule your most time-sensitive and essential tasks during times when you know you'll be able to operate at peak efficiency.

Scheduling a time-sensitive or essential task for 4 P.M. on a Friday (when you clock out at 5 P.M.) is not the best idea. You'll already be tired and probably thinking about your upcoming weekend.

Again, while it makes sense to preplan each workday, you always need to be able to pivot and refocus your attention on an unscheduled but time-sensitive task when it crops up. For this reason, try to avoid cramming every minute of your workday with time-sensitive tasks. In addition to your breaks, schedule a few 30-minute periods for focusing on essential, important, or nonessential tasks—that way you can replace them with an unplanned essential task if necessary. In other words, learn to build flexibility into your daily or weekly schedule.

### Remote Work Typically Means No More Commute Time

For many people, remote work means eliminating their daily commute. Not only does this save money in gas, tolls, and parking, but it also frees up time—up to several hours each day.

If you're switching to remote work, calculate how much time each day you spent commuting back and forth to the office. Then figure out a productive or meaningful way to use this newfound time in your daily schedule. Some people use the added time to get a head start on work. Others find it beneficial to spend more time with family or pets. You, however, may benefit most by making it "me time."

This is time in your day that you set aside for yourself. It could be a time when you exercise, meditate, participate in a hobby, get personal stuff done around your home, read, listen to a podcast, catch up on the daily news, listen to music, or do something else that allows you to take your mind off work and other responsibilities. You can also allocate this time to expanding your professional skill set or participating in other types of educational or enrichment activities that over time will make you a more valuable employee and allow you to earn more money.

You should still schedule this time into your calendar (as "personal time" or "me time"). However, once you allocate this time, it's important to use it the way you meant it to be used. Spending as little as 15 to 30 minutes every morning and every afternoon to clear your mind, do something active, or participate in an activity you enjoy will go a long way toward reducing stress, preventing burnout, and allowing you to explore opportunities for personal growth.

### Proven Time Management Tools

The time management tools you adopt will become indispensable in your everyday life. For this reason, if you use a digital scheduling tool, make sure it will sync between your computer(s), smartphone, tablet, and smartwatch (if you have one) via the cloud. Set up these devices to generate appropriate alerts, alarms, and notifications throughout your workday.

Be sure to use the same calendar/scheduling app as your co-workers or teammates, so you can share and sync your schedules (when appropriate) and easily schedule meetings. Data compatibility between apps like Microsoft Outlook, Google Calendar, and Apple Calendar can be tricky.

For a remote worker, using an old school paper planner or calendar is not typically efficient for multiple reasons. You can't back up and sync your calendar, and you can't easily share aspects of your schedule with others. Copying appointments or meeting invitations manually into a paper calendar also increases the chance of errors if you write down the wrong time, date, or appointment/task information. For most people, using a digital calendar or scheduling tool is far more efficient.

Ideally you want to work with just one time management/scheduling/calendar tool. Some of the most popular tools used by remote workers include:

- ⋯▶ *Apple Calendar* (support.apple.com/guide/calendar): This is a free calendar and scheduling application that's built into all Apple Macs, iPhones, and iPads. It also syncs data with the Apple Watch and its iCloud cloud-based service.
- ⋯▶ *Calendly* (calendly.com): This is a cloud-based scheduling tool that is highly customizable and allows you to share your calendar with others so they can remotely schedule appointments, calls, or virtual meetings with you, based on times and days you allocate as available. Some of Calendly's services are free, but a paid monthly subscription (starting at $8 per month, per user) is required to unlock all its features and functionality.
- ⋯▶ *Fantastical* (flexibits.com/fantastical): This calendar/scheduling application is subscription-based (starting at $4.99 per month, per user) and available exclusively for Macs, iPhones, iPads, and the Apple Watch. It does, however, allow data to be synced with all popular calendar services, including iCloud, Google, Microsoft Exchange Calendar, Outlook.com, Microsoft 365, and others.

- *Google Calendar* (calendar.google.com): This is a free, cloud-based scheduling, calendar, and to-do list manager that is available from any internet-connected computer or mobile device. Calendar data can be easily shared with anyone also using Google Calendar (or a compatible application).
- *Microsoft Outlook* (bit.ly/3TbqYUc): This is a free calendar, scheduling, to-do list, and email management app that is part of the Microsoft 365 suite of applications but can also be used on its own. The basic Outlook application is free for all computers and mobile devices, but a more robust, premium version is also available.
- *Monday.com* (monday.com): The scheduling/calendar functionality offered by Monday.com is part of an overall, online tool designed for project management and team management. Basic functionality is free, but a more robust, subscription-based version is available starting at $8 per month, per user.

Depending on your work, you may discover a scheduling/time management application designed specifically for your industry. To find what's available, go to any search engine and enter the search phrase "Best time management application for [insert your industry]."

Meanwhile, if your work responsibilities involve project management, you'll want to use a separate project management application that syncs with your time management tool. Likewise, if your work requires time tracking so you can bill your clients appropriately or show your employer how you spend your time, ideally this feature should be built into your chosen calendar/time management application so you can avoid having to sync or copy data between multiple applications.

## Learn Time Management Skills

If you need to learn how to properly manage your time, a wide range of low-cost, online classes and resources are at your disposal. Some of these include:

- *Managing Your Time* (LinkedIn Learning): bit.ly/3RVNqzK
- *Project and Time Management Training* (SkillPath): bit.ly/3Cr8nwY

 ⋅▷ *Time Management* (Dale Carnegie): bit.ly/3fX48Bz

 ▷ *Time Management Classes* (CreativeLive): cr8.lv/3Vzy1IH

 ⋅▷ *Time Management Fundamentals* (LinkedIn Learning): bit.ly/3g1o6uW

 ▷ *Time Management Training* (Pryor Learning): bit.ly/3CRQh8w

 ⋅▷ *Work Smarter, Not Harder: Time Management for Personal & Professional Productivity* (Coursera): bit.ly/3S4wqaQ

## Become an Effective Collaborator

Being a remote worker does not necessarily mean you're all alone in the corporate universe. You'll often need to collaborate with co-workers, teammates, customers, and clients. This might require working together from different locations on the creation or editing of a document or spreadsheet. It might also mean remotely participating in a brainstorming session.

Whether you're working with others from different remote locations or needing to easily share files in a secure way, you'll have to use a variety of online collaboration tools.

Becoming a highly productive and effective collaborator will typically require you to become proficient using a collection of cloud-based tools for messaging, project management, email, document collaboration, and file sharing. It's essential that you and your employer, as well as your co-workers or teammates, all agree on what tools will be used to ensure full compatibility. You'll also need to develop proper etiquette for using these tools.

Chapter 6, "How to Remotely Collaborate," focuses on some of the most common cloud-based collaboration tools used by remote workers, offers resources for becoming proficient using them, and will help you develop the proper etiquette to communicate clearly and effectively (without infringing on other people's personal time or interfering in their daily schedule).

In addition to choosing the most appropriate collaboration tools, you must learn how to use them securely, so that confidential or highly sensitive information does not get hacked or leaked to the wrong people. The most common cause of these types of data breaches or leaks is human error.

Many of the applications you already know and use, such as all the applications that are part of Microsoft 365, Google Workspace, and Apple iWork. Evernote, Dropbox, Slack, Trello, and Zoom also have built-in collaboration tools. These integrated tools allow you to share files with other people or collaborate on the creation or editing of documents and other files in real time and from remote locations.

However, knowing how to set up a secure internet connection and when and how to password protect, encrypt, and share permissions with other people will be essential. If you don't understand how to activate file permissions so co-workers or collaborators can access specific files, you'll wind up wasting a lot of time communicating back and forth and later tinkering with those settings.

Also, when using these tools, you have the option of collaborating in real time or taking turns reviewing or editing files at each person's convenience. If you opt to collaborate in real time, you'll need to schedule convenient times to work together. You'll also want to create agendas and goals and set a time limit for each real-time collaboration session.

Then once you get past the initial pleasantries, you'll all need to focus on the task at hand, avoid distractions, and avoid going off on unproductive tangents. You'll also need to listen to and respect other people's ideas and opinions, provide constructive criticism (but only when it's appropriate), and gain the respect of those you're working with while showing them the same level of professionalism and respect you want to receive yourself.

Ultimately, collaborating with others is more than just sharing raw data and knowledge. It's about focusing on the same task or goal, working together to achieve each objective, supporting each other, and making the experience as straightforward and easy as possible for everyone involved.

Once you determine which tools you and your collaborators will use, learn how to use them on your own, so you don't waste everyone else's time. The company that developed the collaboration tool you'll be using likely offers free online tutorials and instructional videos you can take advantage of.

Remember, though, that cloud-based collaboration tools are continuously evolving. With each new product update, you'll discover new features and functionality you may be expected to begin using immediately, as well as changes to the user interface you'll need to adapt to. One of your ongoing responsibilities is to be prepared for and be able to use the new updates as they're made available to ensure the productivity of your entire team.

Remember, it's your job as a remote worker to make sure you have all the equipment and resources you'll need to effectively communicate and complete your work responsibilities. Chapter 4, "How to Set Up and Organize Your Home or Remote Office," will help you gather the equipment and tools you'll need. Focus on learning how to use this equipment, while making sure everything is compatible with your co-workers and employer.

## Prepare Yourself to Work Remotely

If you're transitioning from being a traditional office worker to working remotely, in addition to developing the skills we've outlined in this chapter, you'll likely need to adapt your existing work habits and workflow to accommodate your new situation. How to adjust to this new style of working is the focus of the next chapter.

## CHAPTER 3

# Adapting Your Existing Work Habits and Workflow to Remote Working

aking the transition to becoming a successful and productive remote worker might mean having to change your work schedule, work habits, and overall workflow. In fact, you'll likely need to focus on scheduling your time, altering the way you communicate and collaborate, and taking on a more digital approach to managing your paperwork. You'll also probably need to become less reliant on the in-person support staff and services offered by your employer or team and discover how to use your computers and mobile devices more effectively.

## Identify and Outline Your Existing Work Responsibilities

While your core work responsibilities likely won't change much as a remote worker, what will change is how you approach, organize, and ultimately complete your assignments. So take another look at your original job description and then think about how you typically spend your days working from a traditional office or other work environment. Compile a comprehensive list of your responsibilities and how you approach each of them.

Invest a few minutes on Figure 3.1 below to help you describe your top responsibilities and how much time you spend managing them. Also consider what in-office tools, applications, and resources you currently require.

FIGURE 3.1—**Define Your Core Work Responsibilities**

| Work Responsibility | Your Approach | In-Office Tools and Resources Used | Supervisor, Support Staff, and/or Team Members You Collaborate With |
|---|---|---|---|
|  |  |  |  |
|  |  |  |  |
|  |  |  |  |
|  |  |  |  |
|  |  |  |  |
|  |  |  |  |
|  |  |  |  |
|  |  |  |  |

As you move forward as a remote worker, consider that the In-Office Tools and Resources Used column in Figure 3.1 is no longer readily available to you. Thus you'll need to gather the appropriate equipment, software, and supplies for your new work location (whether that's a home office, shared work space, café, or hotel room). The applications you will be using may or may not be dictated by your employer. If you're a freelancer, for example, you may need to adapt to using a different set of tools for each of your clients. Or depending on your work responsibilities, it may be left up to you to determine which applications will work best for you or your team. While your employer, if applicable, may provide you with a company computer, it might be your responsibility to equip the rest of your home or remote office with the specific tools you need to get your job done—such as a smartphone, tablet, and specific type of printer.

Next, looking at each of your core responsibilities, figure out who in your traditional office setting you needed to answer to, collaborate with, or turn to for support. How will you continue to interact with these people (e.g., through email, text messaging, video calls, virtual meetings, or online collaboration tools)? As you figure out your new approach, make sure you're on the same page as everyone else on your team. It's essential that you all use the same tools and applications so you can continue working closely together, albeit from different locations. Again, depending on the type of work you do, your employment situation (full-time, contractor, freelancer, etc.), your employer, and your work responsibilities, the applications or tools you'll be using may or may not be chosen for you.

The in-person daily meetings previously held in your office's conference room will now need to be held virtually, using Zoom (zoom.us), Microsoft Teams (microsoft.com/en-us/microsoft-teams/), Google Meet (meet.google.com), FaceTime (apple.co/3CSeHyV), or another popular virtual meeting application.

One-on-one communication with superiors, co-workers, team members, or support staff will now need to be conducted via telephone, video call, text messaging, or online collaboration tool. Meanwhile, any paperwork that was previously shared in an office setting will now need to be handled digitally. Not only will you need to get used to creating, viewing, organizing, and sharing digital files (such as PDF or Word documents), you'll also need to pay attention to permissions, file-specific passwords, and other security tools to make sure only the right people have access to certain files.

Unfortunately, for most remote workers, there isn't one go-to application that'll handle all these needs. This means you'll likely have to use a combination of text messaging, email, online collaboration, and cloud-based file sharing tools. Some of the most common ones include Slack (slack.com), Microsoft 365 (office.com), and Google Workspace (workspace.google.com/business).

Again, it's essential that you pinpoint a select group of tools to use that everyone has access to, that are approved by your employer, and that offer appropriate security protocols. New procedures and etiquette for creating, distributing, responding to, and working with something as basic as an interoffice memo will need to be established, as well as when it's appropriate to communicate through text messaging or file sharing, as opposed to a phone call, a one-on-one video call, or a group virtual meeting.

As you develop your new way of working, collaborating, and communicating with your superiors, team members, and support staff, remember that everyone's time is valuable. Instead of making an unscheduled phone call, potentially interrupting someone else's day or having to play phone tag, consider less intrusive and more efficient ways to communicate and share information. At the very least, develop a process for scheduling calls, meetings, and interactions across your team, and adjust your scheduling and time management accordingly.

## Adapt Your Company's Workflow to Support a Remote Work Situation

Just as you have your own way of doing things that make you efficient at your job, your company likely has established ways of doing things that might have been developed years ago—long before remote working was common, or even possible. If your employer does not already have processes and procedures in place for their remote workers, it'll be their responsibility to establish remote working protocols and security procedures, as well as dictate which tools you'll ultimately use.

However, smaller companies without an IT department may rely more on their remote working employees to come together and help establish the necessary protocols and procedures. When this occurs, it's common for each individual team within an organization to develop its own workflow and its own set of tools. Then when teams need to interact or individuals from different teams need to exchange information, compatibility issues tend to arise.

One of the biggest challenges in transitioning from a traditional office to a remote situation is that most, if not all, of the required changes in your workflow, scheduling, file sharing, and communication methods need to happen immediately. There's often no time to adjust to the transition or create an efficient remote work space.

If your last day working from a traditional office is on Friday, by the following Monday you'll need to be up and running from your remote work space. Preplanning as much as possible, and investing the time in advance to learn the tools and applications you'll be relying on, is essential.

One of the biggest time wasters is not having tested your remote video call or virtual meeting equipment, so everyone needs to wait for you to get your webcam, microphone, lighting, and/or software working properly. This becomes even more of a challenge if you need to switch between apps and minor bugs prevent the webcam or microphone from working correctly.

Also remember that in addition to just being seen and heard during a video call or virtual meeting, you'll often need to share your screen to present content, share files with others, break out into smaller groups, or use a virtual whiteboard—all of which require tools you'll need to master right away.

Adopting an "I'll learn as I go" approach seldom works in this situation. Any time you spend trying to figure things out on the fly winds up wasting other people's time, which frustrates everyone. To keep things running smoothly, have a backup plan in place for each common process or procedure, so you know what to do when something doesn't go as planned.

What happens when, five minutes before an important virtual meeting, your internet goes down? What if your primary computer crashes during an important part of your workday or work week? While most of the online communication, virtual meeting, and file sharing tools used by remote workers are extremely reliable, what happens if one of them goes down? You need answers to all these questions, and more.

## When It Comes to Internet Access, Have a Backup Plan

As a remote worker, continuous access to a reliable, high-speed, and secure internet connection is essential. But if your primary internet connection goes down, you still need to get online. Make sure you can use a personal wifi hotspot generated by your smartphone or a separate personal wifi hotspot device, so you can continue working while your main internet connection is out of commission. If that's not an option, grab your laptop and work from a library, coffee shop, or hotel lobby that has a public wifi hotspot you can use until your regular connection is restored.

If you can't currently create a personal wifi hotspot from your smartphone (and have a plan that offers unlimited cellular data usage), consider upgrading your cellular service now, before an emergency hits and you must scramble to get it activated.

Two other alternatives for a backup internet connection at home or when working from any location outside your office are to acquire a tablet with its own 5G cellular data connectivity or purchase a stand-alone mobile wifi hotspot device that you can activate on a per-day basis, with no monthly fees.

The Solis Lite (soliswifi.co) is one example of a mobile hotspot device. You buy it outright for less than $200. You then purchase daily, flat-rate internet access passes (for less than $10 per day) that can be used to connect up to 10 devices to the internet, from virtually anywhere within the United States or in more than 140 countries around the world. Monthly subscription plans are also available if you'll need to use the device more frequently. Many similar devices are available, from companies like AT&T Wireless, Verizon, T-Mobile, Netgear, GlocalMe, and Net10. Ideally, you want a mobile hotspot that offers 5G connectivity, although devices that still rely on a slower 4G LTE cellular data connection are more affordable.

## 11 Strategies for Making a Smooth Transition to Working from Home

The following strategies will help you make the smoothest possible transition to working remotely, or become even more efficient if you're already doing it. Many of these strategies are covered in much greater detail elsewhere in the book, but they're all things you should be considering right from the start.

### 1. Set Established Work Hours, But Remain Flexible

The line between personal time and work time will blur when you become a remote worker. In fact, especially if you're loyal to your employer, you'll be inclined to work extra hours and catch up on loose ends during nights, weekends, and holidays. Resist this instinct.

Yes, you want to be readily accessible if there's a true work emergency. However, the trick to managing a balance between your personal and professional life is to do your best to maintain scheduled work hours. Make it clear that you're available via email, text message, phone calls, etc. during your workday, but that you won't respond to unimportant communications during your off-hours.

Until you've developed a routine and become proficient with the new applications and tools you need to do your job, putting in some paid or unpaid overtime may be required. Moving forward, however, it becomes your responsibility to create that all-important distinction between your personal and professional life.

If it's a Saturday afternoon and you're supposed to be watching your child's Little League game, but you're sitting at the field reading emails on your smartphone, you have not yet found the balance between your work and personal life. And this is something your family, friends, and even your pets will likely notice and find disappointing and frustrating.

### 2. Create a Daily Schedule for Yourself, Complete with To-Do Lists

Becoming fully responsible for your time can be a challenge, especially early on in your remote work transition. As discussed in Chapter 2, "Being a Successful Remote Worker Is a Skill Set unto Itself," mastering the art of time management will require planning, scheduling, and attentiveness.

In addition to blocking out how you plan to spend each day using some type of calendar or scheduling app, preferably one that allows you to share your schedule with your superiors and team members (and vice versa), many people find it extremely useful to maintain one or more to-do lists to help keep them focused and on task.

Depending on your work habits, you may find it beneficial to keep one master to-do list with all your prioritized daily, weekly, monthly, and long-term objectives. However, some people find a project management application that combines scheduling with to-do list management more useful. Others find working with multiple, project-specific to-do lists fits better into their workflow.

Whichever tools or methodology you use, at the end of each day, invest 15 minutes to create a schedule that includes prioritized to-do list items for the following workday. This allows you to begin each day with a clear set of objectives and enables you to take a more organized approach to completing each required task.

### 3. Create the Best Possible Remote Work Space

One of the biggest benefits to being a remote worker is that in most cases, you can fully personalize your work space. As you'll see in Chapter 4, "How to Set Up and Organize Your Home or Remote Office," this is different from simply gathering all the equipment, applications, and tools you need for your job.

Instead, creating the best possible remote work space includes choosing the best location from which to work—you should consider noise levels, décor, potential distractions, temperature, ergonomics, power requirements (such as electrical outlets), and lighting. Something as simple as a work space that's too hot or cold or not properly lit can have a huge impact on your productivity, physical comfort, and mental state.

If you'll be working from home, you'll have a lot more options for customizing your work space than if you're using a shared work space. However, you can choose a shared work space that meets your needs and personal preferences. This also applies if you'll be working remotely from public locations, like a coffee shop, hotel, airport, or library. You can often choose a space that is out of the way (to avoid noise and distractions) and that offers proper lighting.

Whether you're choosing and personalizing a long-term work space or selecting a remote work location you'll be using for just a few hours, think about what you need from that space, choose it wisely, and then customize it to the best of your abilities.

### 4. Figure Out What New Expenses Your Employer Will Cover

Another tremendous benefit of becoming a remote worker is that you'll potentially save a lot of money and time when it comes to commuting, parking, and going out for lunch and coffee. However, new expenses will arise that partially offset these savings.

As you set up your home office, you'll likely need to purchase a desk, office chair, home office printer, and other equipment. Your home electric bill will potentially go up, because you'll be running more equipment that requires power. You'll probably also need to upgrade your home's internet and wifi connectivity and encounter other potential expenses.

If possible, before you make the transition to remote work, talk to your employer about what expenses will be covered, so you can better budget for any one-time or ongoing expenses you'll incur.

While your employer might provide you with a laptop computer, depending on the work you'll be doing and where you'll be working, you might want to use a portable or second full-size monitor with your laptop to increase your screen size and more easily view multiple applications at once. You might also need an all-in-one printer (with a photocopier and scanner), plus an assortment of applications that require a one-time purchase or ongoing subscription fee to use.

As you read Chapter 4, think about what equipment, applications, office furniture, and tools you'll need, so that when you open a dialogue with your employer, you'll have a clearly defined budget for acquiring everything you'll need—right down to a stapler with staples. Even if you're not going to be working from home, there is a monthly fee (plus additional expenses) for using a shared work space. And even if you plan to work from airports while traveling, you might find you're much more productive working from an airport lounge (which has a per-visit or annual fee for entry).

Determining in advance what your employer will cover will help you avoid the unpleasant surprise of work-related bills—and ease the strain on your personal budget.

## 5. Invest in the Right Technology

In addition to creating a work space that's comfortable, ergonomic, and as distraction-free as possible, it's essential to choose the technology, applications, tools, and equipment that'll allow you to get your work done. We've emphasized this point multiple times throughout this book because, as a remote worker, you'll likely develop a very strong reliance on technology. Focusing on compatibility and security and keeping all applications up-to-date will be an ongoing responsibility.

## 6. Discuss Expectations, Policies, and Procedures with Your Employer

Especially with the COVID-19 pandemic lasting for so long, most employers have been forced to develop company-wide policies and procedures for remote workers. In addition to making sure you understand and can follow these policies, be sure to discuss their and your expectations in advance.

You'll want to agree to what consists of a typical workday and what you're expected to accomplish each day. Your discussion should cover:

- How you'll communicate
- Ways you'll share files using the cloud
- Etiquette for using various communication and collaboration tools
- How you'll handle scheduling and time tracking

Your team leader may require you to attend all virtual meetings with your camera turned on and dress in appropriate, business-friendly attire. And while you may be required to maintain a standard 9 A.M. to 5 P.M. workday, there needs to be an easy way for someone to reach you after-hours if a work emergency arises. Make sure you define what a "work emergency" is.

Ideally, all your company's remote work policies and procedures should be given to you in writing. You should also document any additional agreements you make with your employer regarding expectations of how day-to-day activities will be handled. Throughout your remote work experience, maintaining continuous, clear communication with your employer, co-workers, teammates, support staff, customers, clients, and anyone else you do business with will remain essential.

### 7. Maintain a Virtual Paper Trail for All Aspects of Your Work

It's one thing to say you're doing something. It's another thing altogether to be able to document how you spent your time, what you accomplished, your achievements, and what conversations or communications you've had and with whom. Keep in mind that virtually all the communication, file sharing, scheduling, and collaboration tools you'll be working with maintain detailed records: recordings, copies of files, transcripts of verbal communications, and backups of all electronic communications (emails, text messages, etc.)—which your employer typically has full access to.

However, you should also get into the habit of keeping detailed records of what you do, when you do it, how you did it, and any other pertinent information. Remember, your employer or supervisor will no longer be able to physically see you working each day. If a miscommunication, mistake, technological glitch, or other problem arises, you may need to be able to refer to your own records to account for your actions, address the issue, or fix the situation in a timely manner.

Of course, developing a system that anticipates and works to avoid any complications is ideal, but unexpected problems do arise. Be prepared to deal with these issues properly and effectively.

### 8. Pay Attention to Your Mental and Physical Needs

Part of creating the proper work space for you is making sure it takes care of your mental health and physical needs on an ongoing basis.

First, this requires you to get to know yourself and what your personal needs are. Then take steps to ensure you're meeting those needs every day. This means using ergonomic office furniture and equipment to avoid muscle aches, tension, and strain. It also means working in a space that's well-lit and a comfortable temperature, and that offers plenty of fresh air.

Get in the habit of taking a break every hour or two to stand up and stretch. Avoid staring at a computer screen for hours on end, and go for a walk or do something else physical midday. To reduce eyestrain, look away from your computer screen for a full 20 seconds every hour. Taking the time to eat a proper lunch away from your desk and breaking up monotonous tasks will also help your physical and mental health.

Take steps in advance to combat loneliness and isolation (which is often a side effect of remote working) and maintain personal friendships with your co-workers that you don't see daily or work side by side with (in a traditional sense).

Nobody knows you better than you do. Decide what you need to stay happy, healthy, focused, motivated, and productive working remotely, and then take planned steps to address your needs. This is something few employers can or will do on your behalf.

### 9. Exchange Remote Work Strategies with Your Co-Workers

Whatever challenges or obstacles you face as a remote worker will likely also be experienced by your co-workers. At the same time, whatever work habits you adopt, tools or applications you identify as being useful, or remote work strategies that turn out to be beneficial will likely also help them. Get into the habit of discussing your remote work habits and sharing photos (or short video tours) of your respective remote work spaces. Share details about what furniture, equipment, tools, and applications you use, and share solutions to problems you've encountered.

Setting up opportunities to informally share ideas, strategies, and solutions about remote working will benefit everyone. These interactions can even be used as team bonding experiences, because everyone on your team will likely face the same issues and challenges—and be looking for ways to overcome them.

### 10. Maintain Continuous and Clear Communication with Your Managers and Team

Because you'll no longer be working side by side with your managers, it's essential to maintain continuous and clear communication with them, following procedures and etiquette that everyone has agreed to. This means you should tell your superiors where you are, what you're doing, and how you're doing it. Especially if you encounter a problem or delay, make the appropriate people aware of the situation immediately and then work together to overcome whatever challenges you encounter. In any work situation, information is power. When everyone has the information they need, things can get done more effectively and smoothly.

## 11. Create or Participate in Remote Social or Team-Building Activities

Just because people have started to work remotely, your company's unique, preexisting culture doesn't have to die. When you're working remotely, chitchatting with a co-worker in an adjacent cubicle, gathering at the water cooler during a break, going out to lunch with your best friend from work, or sitting around a conference table and shooting the breeze before a meeting are no longer possible.

But there are still plenty of ways to maintain a personal connection with the people you work with—assuming everyone is willing to put in the effort. Consider encouraging your employer to plan virtual or in-person gatherings that revolve around social time and team-building exercises. You should also schedule some occasions on your own with your work friends to socialize (in person or virtually). Within your organization, consider establishing a social committee that meets weekly or biweekly to plan virtual or in-person activities for all employees or teammates at least once per month.

Something as simple as gathering in a virtual meeting to celebrate someone's birthday, hosting a virtual baby shower for an expecting mother, or sending a get well card (electronically or in the mail) when a co-worker is sick are all activities that will help you develop and maintain a personal connection with the people you work with—even if you're not seeing them face-to-face every day. By using technology, creativity, and the resources at your disposal, it's easier than ever for you and your co-workers to interact socially, in both formal and informal ways. Punchbowl.com (punchbowl.com/ecards/get-well) is an example of an online service that allows you to send customized get well cards electronically.

To help you get started, go to any internet search engine and enter the phrase "remote team-building activities." You'll discover websites and free online guides that are chock-full of strategies and ideas you can use—even with little to no budget. To name just one, Gallup publishes a free annual report, "The Guide to Employee Engagement." You can download the 2022 version at gallup.com/workplace/. Meanwhile, hundreds of companies, like Wildgoose (wearewildgoose.com/usa/), specialize in hosting team-building activities, and many of them have added virtual and hybrid (a mix of virtual and in-person) activities to their roster.

Other low-cost (or free) ways to promote team building and social interactions between co-workers include:

- ▸ Set up a virtual break room that's accessible to everyone before and after work hours and during lunch, where people can gather online and socialize. This can be done easily via a Slack channel, for example.
- ▸ Have everyone share photos or short videos of their remote work spaces.
- ▸ Schedule a weekly meeting where everyone shares something positive or exciting from their personal lives, whether it's introducing everyone to their pets, showing photos from recent vacations, or sharing details about their hobbies.
- ▸ Through emails or text messaging, create an open forum to congratulate people on professional or personal accomplishments and acknowledge birthdays, anniversaries, and other important dates.
- ▸ Schedule monthly or quarterly virtual team learning sessions where someone (either from your company or from elsewhere) offers a one-hour, upbeat tutorial or class. This could cover a work-related topic or something more fun, like wine pairing, a chocolate tasting, a trivia challenge, a virtual murder mystery, a painting class, a bonsai tree growing class, or a cooking demonstration. These can all be done using virtual meeting tools at your disposal.
- ▸ Create an online forum where people can post fun and candid photos of themselves, their pets, and/or their family.
- ▸ Once or twice per month, plan a virtual group lunch hour. Using your usual virtual meeting platform, everyone can enjoy a boxed or preordered lunch while you socialize for 30 to 60 minutes. During this time, the team can break into two or more groups and participate in a trivia challenge. For instance, Ricotta (ricotta.team/), available for Slack, offers a collection of free and subscription-based icebreaker games and team-building activities. The employer can offer a $25 reimbursement for a lunch, or arrange for a DoorDash gift certificate or a gift certificate to a chain restaurant or supermarket (like Whole Foods).

## Make a Smooth Transition to Working from Anywhere

Whether you choose to work from a home office or a shared work space, you'll need to gather the necessary equipment and tools, learn to use them, and become accustomed to your new environment and workflow.

The same is true if you'll be working from other remote locations (such as a coffee shop, airport, hotel, or library), but you'll have less control over your work space. You will, however, have full control over the equipment you use, so make sure you have everything you need. This might include carrying around your own power strip or a portable, battery-powered unit that will keep your computer and mobile devices running all day.

To avoid distractions when working in public, noise-cancelation headphones may become an essential business tool. Connecting a portable monitor to your laptop will allow you to view and work with several applications at once. To ensure you always have access to the internet, you might find that a mobile hotspot is essential; if you need to print and scan while on the go, a portable printer might be necessary as well.

With a bit of creativity and planning, a skilled remote worker can get their work done from almost anywhere. The key is to travel with gear that can be set up quickly and that allows you to be productive, even without access to an electrical outlet or public wifi hotspot.

## Start By Creating Your Ideal Work Space

Again, beyond just having a continuous, reliable, and high-speed internet connection, as well as the right collection of tools and applications, it's essential to create a personalized workplace for yourself that will allow you to be as productive as possible—one that's clean, comfortable, climate-controlled, well-lit, quiet, aesthetically pleasing, and ergonomic.

Whether you'll be working from home, from a shared work space, or from a café, hotel room, airport, or anywhere else, the focus of the next chapter is on helping you create the ideal work space and environment for working remotely.

# How to Set Up and Organize Your Home or Remote Office

One of the most important components of becoming a successful remote worker, regardless of your occupation, is creating a well-equipped and well-organized work space that's conducive to your work habits and needs. In other words, you should not adapt too much to your available work space. Instead, make the work space you select suitable for you.

In this chapter, you'll find that where you work is as important as the equipment and tools at your disposal. Things like spaciousness, lighting, temperature, air quality, ambient sounds, internet connection, electrical outlets, and distractions will all impact your ability to work efficiently.

That said, you also need the right tools and equipment to get your work done. And you'll need to develop appropriate work habits and remote working skills, based on whether you're working from home, in a coffee shop or other public space, or from a shared work space not associated with your employer.

Regardless of which space you choose, this chapter will help you create the most suitable and well-organized work environment possible. You'll also discover how to equip your work space with the tools, equipment, and applications you'll likely need—without spending a fortune.

## Identify the Perfect Work Space Within Your Home

Some people have an extra room in their home that they can use as a customized home office. If that's the case for you, consider yourself very lucky! Most people who wind up working from home, however, need to reallocate space that's already being used for something else.

And for those who are really tight on living space, it may be necessary to set up your work space each day, and then revert that space back to your bedroom, dining room, or living room once the workday ends. Logistically, this is the least desirable situation, but sometimes you have to live with it.

The following chart (Figure 4.1) lists the most common rooms and spaces in a home where people set up their home office as well as some of the pros and cons related to those spaces.

FIGURE 4.1—**Choosing the Location for Your Home Office**

| Room Type | Pros | Cons |
|---|---|---|
| Attic | Private | Poor air quality |
| | | Lack of space (low ceilings) |
| | | Poor accessibility |
| | | Already used for storage |
| | | Possible mold and/or mildew |

FIGURE 4.1—**Choosing the Location for Your Home Office,** cont.

| Room Type | Pros | Cons |
|---|---|---|
| Attic, cont. | | Possible weak wifi signal |
| | | Lack of electrical outlets |
| | | Poor lighting |
| Basement | Private and spacious | Poor air quality |
| | | Poor accessibility |
| | | Already used for storage |
| | | Floors and ceilings may be unfinished |
| | | Possible mold and/or mildew |
| | | Possible weak wifi signal |
| | | Lack of electrical outlets |
| | | No temperature control |
| | | Poor lighting |
| Dining Room | Climate-controlled (easy to adjust the temperature) | Lack of privacy |
| | Spacious | Must set up and take down your office whenever it will be used for eating |
| | Well-lit (with natural light and lighting fixtures) | |
| Garage | Spacious | Where will you put your car(s)? |
| | | Lack of climate control (may be too cold in the winter) |
| | | Poor lighting |
| | | Possible mold and/or mildew |
| | | Poor air quality |
| | | Floors, ceilings, and walls may be unfinished |
| | | Difficult to decorate |
| | | Possible weak wifi signal |
| | | Lack of electrical outlets |

FIGURE 4.1—**Choosing the Location for Your Home Office,** cont.

| Room Type | Pros | Cons |
|---|---|---|
| Guest Bedroom | Spacious<br><br>Climate-controlled<br><br>Well-lit (with windows and natural light)<br><br>Strong wifi signal<br><br>Accessible electrical outlets<br><br>Private | You'll need to pack up your "office" when you have company overnight |
| Kitchen Counter | Climate-controlled | Lack of space<br><br>You must keep it extra clean<br><br>You'll need to pack up your office daily<br><br>Many distractions (from people and appliances)<br><br>You can't work from a traditional desk or use a comfortable office chair |
| Part of a Living Room | Climate-controlled<br><br>Accessible electrical outlets<br><br>Strong wifi signal | Work-life balance is more difficult<br><br>Many potential distractions<br><br>Lack of space for a traditional desk and comfortable office chair<br><br>You may need to pack up your office daily |
| Part of a Master Bedroom | Private<br><br>Well-lit (windows)<br><br>Climate-controlled<br><br>Strong wifi signal<br><br>Accessible electrical outlets | You'll be working where you sleep—poor work-life balance<br><br>No space for a desk, office chair, and office equipment<br><br>You may need to work around a spouse's or roommate's sleep schedule |

FIGURE 4.1—**Choosing the Location for Your Home Office,** cont.

| Room Type | Pros | Cons |
|---|---|---|
| Spare Room | Spacious<br>You can easily redecorate<br>Climate-controlled<br>Accessible electrical outlets<br>Private<br>Strong wifi signal<br>Fewer distractions<br>Good lighting | If this room was previously used for storage or another purpose, those contents will need to be relocated |
| Walk-In Closet | Private | Lack of space<br>Poor lighting (no windows)<br>Poor ventilation<br>Lack of electrical outlets<br>Less storage space in your home |

## 10 Considerations When Choosing Where to Set Up Your Home Office

When choosing the location of your home office, here are 10 important points to consider:

### 1. Accessibility to Electrical Outlets

For safety and aesthetic reasons, if you have many devices to plug in or keep charged, you don't want to rely on multiple extension cords or power strips plugged into a single electrical outlet. Power cables stretching across the floor of a room or between rooms is unsightly and potentially dangerous (especially if you have young kids or pets).

Make sure your work space has an adequate number of electrical outlets and power strips with surge protectors. Surge protectors are especially important for your computer and other high-end electronics. If your power goes out often, consider investing in an uninterruptible power supply, at least for your computer.

## 2. Air Quality

If your work space contains mold or mildew or is musty due to lack of natural light and ventilation, not only can the air be unsafe to breathe, but it will also create an unpleasant work environment. If your work space can't have a steady flow of fresh air, consider adding an air purifier. Depending on the local climate, you may also need a humidifier or dehumidifier, as well as a quiet fan to circulate air throughout the room.

## 3. Ambient Sounds

Every room has ambient sounds. Before setting up your work space, walk into the middle of the room, close your eyes and stand still, and spend several minutes focusing just on what you hear. Are these sounds annoying, distracting, or overpowering? What can be done to muffle or eliminate the outside sounds in this space (such as the sound of nearby traffic, birds chirping, machinery running, dogs barking, or TVs playing)?

Would adding carpeting to the floor or acoustic panels to the walls or ceiling help to create a quieter, more functional work space? Sure, you can wear noise-canceling headphones, but this is not a long-term solution for ongoing noise issues.

Many companies, offer affordable acoustic paneling that can reduce or eliminate unwanted sound within a room like Acoustics America (acousticsamerica.com/product-space/residential).

## 4. Décor

The décor of your work space will go a long way toward helping to maintain a positive and relaxed mood. Adding one or more houseplants or artwork that you find visually appealing will be helpful. However, choosing matching office furniture, painting the walls a cheerful color, and creating a bright and uplifting atmosphere is also important.

Consider adding a digital picture frame to your desk or wall. Have it display a slideshow of your favorite photos featuring your loved ones, friends, pets, and most memorable vacation moments. At the same time, keep your work space as well-organized and clutter-free as possible.

While you need to be able to work, concentrate, and be productive in your home office, it should also be a place where you can be relaxed, comfortable, and surrounded by art, photos, or knickknacks that make you happy.

## 5. Internet Connection

As a remote worker, you'll rely heavily on the internet. While a wired connection between your computer and modem (or router) can improve your connection speed, this is only practical if your main computer is close to the modem/router. Otherwise, you'll probably rely on a wireless, or wifi, internet connection.

First, contact your internet service provider (ISP) and make sure you're receiving the fastest internet connection speed possible and that you have the most up-to-date modem available from that ISP. Next, evaluate your wireless router, again making sure the technology is current and that it can handle the maximum internet speed offered by your ISP.

Especially if you have more than one person working from home or have kids who will be streaming videos and playing online games while you're having virtual meetings, having a fast internet connection and the latest equipment will be essential.

A variety of free tools are available online that allow you to quickly measure your actual internet connection speed, including:

- *Fast*: fast.com
- *Fusion Connect*: speakeasy.net/speedtest/
- *HighSpeedInternet.com*: highspeedinternet.com/tools/speed-test
- *Speedtest*: speedtest.net/
- *TestMy.net*: testmy.net

The standard for high-speed home internet services is constantly improving. If your equipment is more than two or three years old, chances are you'll want to upgrade it to ensure you're achieving the fastest connection speeds possible from your ISP.

When setting up your internet service, focus on online security. In addition to the firewall offered by your ISP for your modem, invest in anti-virus and malware protection software for your computers, and if you'll be relying on a wifi internet connection, add a virtual private network (VPN) to your computers and mobile devices as well. Use these security tools even if your employer doesn't provide or mandate them.

Antivirus and malware protection applications for Windows PCs and Macs typically have an annual subscription fee. Plan on paying between $30 and $50 per year to protect one to five computers and mobile devices. The following are a few popular options:

- *Bitdefender*: bitdefender.com/
- *McAfee*: mcafee.com/
- *Norton*: us.norton.com/
- *Trend Micro*: trendmicro.com/en_us/business.html

Malwarebytes (malwarebytes.com/) is a powerful antivirus and malware protection application specifically for Macs.

A virtual private network (VPN) is used mainly when connecting to the internet via wifi. This type of technology will automatically encrypt everything you're doing while accessing the internet while also hiding your location. This makes it much harder for hackers to intercept your data and steal your information.

Many VPN services are available, which charge a monthly or annual fee that covers all your computers and mobile devices. Some VPNs also offer added features, like an ad blocker, tracking prevention, and/or a password manager. Like antivirus and malware protection software, setting up a VPN takes just minutes, and once it's activated, it works behind-the-scenes to provide you with an added level of security and privacy when using the internet. We'll focus more on online security and privacy in Chapter 8, "Effectively Deal with Online Security and Privacy Issues."

## 6. Lighting

The lighting in your home office makes a huge difference when it comes to preventing eyestrain, enhancing your concentration, and creating the most comfortable work space possible. Having plenty of natural light via windows and skylights, accompanied by artificial lighting when necessary, is ideal.

Your work area should be surrounded by an even, bright, and steady light source that reduces or eliminates unwanted shadows. If the lighting is too bright or too dim, this will put unnecessary strain on your eyes, as will fluorescent lighting. While direct overhead lighting can fill an entire room with light, it may cause unwanted glare on your computer screens or unwanted shadows over your desk.

Focus on filling your home office with light while eliminating unwanted glare and shadows. In addition to lamps and light sources that flood a large area with light, consider using a desk lamp that allows you to direct a more intense light source to your immediate work area.

Keep in mind that light can also be used for decorative purposes and to add a splash of color to a work space. This decorative lighting should be in addition to the primary lighting in your home office, not in place of it. There are many low-cost, LED smart lighting options, including light strips and accent lights.

A company called Nanoleaf (nanoleaf.me/), for one, offers a nice collection of decorative smart lighting that can be attached to any wall. Meanwhile, companies like Philips Hue (philips-hue.com/) and Govee (us.govee.com) offer collections of smart lights, light strips, and related products that can be used to decorate a home office.

## 7. Localized Distractions

Potential distractions that could keep you from focusing on your work come in many forms: the hum of the air conditioner in your office, the sound of your dog barking or your kids playing, or the noise of airplanes flying overhead, cars driving by, or neighbors talking outside.

Once you determine where you'll be working from, pinpoint the most problematic distractions and figure out how you'll diminish or eliminate their impact. This might include adding a thicker door with a lock to your home office, adding acoustic tiles to the walls or ceiling, or wearing noise-canceling headphones while you work. If you know you will be easily distracted by having a TV or Bluetooth speaker in your office, refrain from adding this equipment.

Because you may already have Apple Music, Spotify, Amazon Music, or Pandora on your smartphone (or easily accessible from your computer), don't allow yourself to listen to music that will be a distraction when you know you need to concentrate on the task at hand. Either avoid music altogether, or choose soft, classical music that won't be a distraction. Again, develop personal discipline based on what you know your work habits should be. Some people work very well with music playing in the background, while for others, this can be a huge distraction. One solution is to create a "work playlist" that only includes soft music that you don't find distracting and then sticking just to that playlist during your workday.

Use Figure 4.2 below to list what you anticipate your top five distractions will be in your home office, and then determine what you need to do to eliminate the problem in advance.

FIGURE 4.2—**Anticipated Distractions and How You'll Eliminate Them**

| Potential Distraction | Cause of the Distraction | Solution for Eliminating the Distraction |
|---|---|---|
| | | |
| | | |
| | | |
| | | |
| | | |
| | | |

## 8. Privacy

Depending on your living situation, privacy can be defined in many ways. If you have roommates, a spouse, a partner, or children, being able to work in a private area may be as simple as choosing a home office with a door that closes and locks.

However, if you need to establish a co-working space with a roommate, partner, or spouse who does not work for the same employer, or if you need to share your work space with your kids once they get home from school, privacy will prove a much greater challenge.

Take a look at the location where you plan to work and figure out what needs to be done to that space to give you the privacy you need. If you can't have an entire room to yourself, perhaps setting up a removable partition or privacy curtain is a viable option. A lot will depend on your personal work habits and the level of privacy you need to get your work done.

Amazon, as well as many companies that sell home office furniture, sells room dividers. These allow for some privacy but do nothing to eliminate noise. Many companies also sell higher-end dividers or modular office cubicles that can be set up in your home. To explore these options, here are some websites to visit:

- *Amazon*: amzn.to/3eobQ7w
- *Fastcubes*: fastcubes.com
- *The Home Depot*: thd.co/3CS3vSL
- *Office Gallery International*: officegallery.net
- *Wayfair*: bit.ly/3RUjxjl

## 9. Spaciousness

Consider the space needed to properly fit your desk, office chair, other office furniture (e.g., file cabinets, a bookcase), and all your work equipment. Ideally, you want your most essential tools and equipment (like your printer and a trash can) within reach. Next, think about how much desk space you need to be productive without having to make too many compromises. Don't settle for a desk that's too small or the wrong height. And don't compromise on your office chair. It should be comfortable, height adjustable, and able to swivel, and provide ample back, neck, and arm support.

One huge mistake is trying to fit too much furniture, too much equipment, and too many supplies into a space that's too small. This could make you feel claustrophobic or surrounded by too much clutter.

## 10. Temperature

Research conducted by several universities, including Cornell, shows that the ideal temperature to maintain in a traditional office filled with people is 77 degrees Fahrenheit, although OSHA recommends keeping the temperature between 68 and 76 degrees. That said, when you're working from home, a lot has to do with your personal preference. While you may have been forced to wear a sweater if the temperature was too cold in your old office, working from home gives you more control over your environment. Temperatures that are too hot or cold will impact your concentration and productivity.

Once you determine the ideal temperature for your work space, figure out the best way to maintain that temperature without overly increasing your home's utility bill. You could add a smart thermostat to your home or place a portable fan or heater in your immediate work space. With a bit of online research, you should be able to find a portable fan or heater that's compact, energy efficient, and quiet. The Dyson Pure Hot + Cool, for instance, serves as a portable heater, fan, and air purifier. If the sun shining through a window generates too much heat, add a window shade or curtains.

While it might take some initial experimentation, and your comfort level at specific temperatures may vary throughout the year, focus on maintaining the ideal temperature for yourself within your work space.

## Home Office Decorating Tips That'll Enhance Your Mood and Productivity

What makes you happy? Consider decorating your office with photos, artwork, or knickknacks that represent your loved ones, pets, friends, fondest memories, and biggest accomplishments. Being surrounded by these images and objects will help you stay motivated and keep you in a positive state of mind—even when work becomes stressful.

Of course, you should avoid too much clutter. However, if you show-case images and items that are important to you, it'll make your work space feel more comforting. Something as simple as making the screen saver on your computer into a slideshow of your favorite family and vacation pho-tos is an impactful way to decorate your home office with minimal effort.

## The Home Office Furniture You'll Likely Need

The centerpiece of your work space should be a spacious, ergonomic, and well-organized desk. If you can't afford something fancy, either look for a used desk being sold online (from Facebook Marketplace, for example) or visit your local IKEA or an office supply superstore. Target and Walmart also sell desks suitable for a home office.

### Choosing the Best Desk for Your Home Office

When choosing your desk, first determine what will be kept on it permanently (such as your desktop computer) and how much space is needed for that equipment, including a keyboard and mouse. Then make sure there's also ample space for you to shuffle papers, use a notepad, or do any other daily work.

Consider the desk design. Would you prefer a traditional rectangular desk, an L-shaped desk with two working surfaces, or a U-shaped desk with three working surfaces? What do you want in terms of desk drawers? Do the drawers need to be lockable? Are you used to working with a separate keyboard drawer or a monitor stand that you'll need space for or want built into your desk?

If you have the budget, you might consider a height-adjustable stand-up desk. According to Uplift Desk's website (upliftdesk.com/), "A growing body of research supports the benefits of standing desks and the myriad of ways they improve your life, from boosting productivity and preventing adverse health conditions caused by sedentary habits to increasing the probability of a pain-free workday by 80 percent."

While you probably don't want to stand up at your desk all day, every day, having an adjustable desk allows you to switch from sitting to standing as often as you want throughout each workday.

### Your Home Office Chair Is an Important Consideration

Again, as important as a desk is, your office chair is equally essential; you should invest whatever you can afford to acquire one that:

- Is height adjustable
- Nicely accommodates your body height and weight with an appropriate seat width and depth
- Provides back/lumbar support
- Offers adjustable and padded armrests

⤳ Swivels and offers the ability to lean back

⤳ Provides comfort and is ergonomically designed

⤳ Is on wheels, so you can move around freely without standing up

⤳ Offers an adjustable headrest

According to Spine-health.com (bit.ly/3TdZgX9), "An ergonomic chair should have a lumbar adjustment (both height and depth) so each user can get the proper fit to support the inward curve of the lower back." It's easy to spend thousands of dollars on a high-end office chair, like a brand-new Herman Miller Aeron chair (bit.ly/3Cqfm9n). However, with a bit of online research, you can find genuine but used Aeron chairs at a fraction of the price. Countless other office chair manufacturers also sell affordable but well-designed, ergonomic, and comfortable seating options.

## Additional Home Office Furniture You May Need

Once you've selected your desk and office chair, gather any remaining home office furniture you might need. Remember to measure your available space before you start shopping. Also think about your former office setup, if applicable, and determine what aspects of it worked well for you and what you would have changed if given the opportunity and budget.

To help you equip your home office, Figure 4.3 below offers a list of furniture and accessories you might want to acquire.

FIGURE 4.3—**Home Office Furniture Worksheet**

| Furniture Type | Required Measurements | Number Required & Notes | Already Have | Need to Purchase |
|---|---|---|---|---|
| Artwork | | | | |
| Bookshelf/Shelves | | | | |
| Desk Accessories | | | | |
| Desk Lamp(s) | | | | |

FIGURE 4.3—**Home Office Furniture Worksheet,** cont.

| Furniture Type | Required Measurements | Number Required & Notes | Already Have | Need to Purchase |
|---|---|---|---|---|
| File Cabinet(s) | | | | |
| Floor Lamp(s) | | | | |
| Floor Protection Mat (aka Chair Mat) | | | | |
| Footrest | | | | |
| Lounge Seating | | | | |
| Monitor Stand | | | | |
| Plant(s) | | | | |
| Printer Stand | | | | |
| Storage Unit(s) (Cabinet) | | | | |
| Trash Can | | | | |
| Wall Clock | | | | |
| Wall Organizer | | | | |
| Whiteboard or Corkboard | | | | |
| Other | | | | |
| Other | | | | |

## Gathering Home Office Equipment to Meet Your Needs

In addition to the home office furniture needed to create a comfortable and productive work space, you'll need to equip that space with appropriate office equipment. Use Figure 4.4 on page 74 to help you gather the equipment you might need, depending on your personal requirements.

FIGURE 4.4—**Home Office Equipment Checklist**

| Home Office Equipment Type | Make/Model and Notes | Already Have | Need to Purchase |
|---|---|---|---|
| Desktop Computer | ☐ Windows PC | | |
| | ☐ Mac | | |
| Desktop Scanner | | | |
| External SSD Hard Drive for Local Data Storage & Backups | | | |
| Laptop Computer | ☐ Windows PC | | |
| | ☐ Mac | | |
| Laptop Computer Docking Station | | | |
| Mobile Device Charging Equipment | | | |
| Modem (for internet) | | | |
| Monitor Antiglare/Privacy Filter | | | |
| Mouse Pad | | | |
| Noise-Cancelation Headphones or Earbuds | | | |
| Paper Shredder | | | |
| Power Strips (with Surge Protector) and Extension Cord(s) | | | |
| Printer (All-in-One Printer/Copier/ Scanner) | ☐ Monochrome Laser Printer | | |
| | ☐ Color Laser Printer | | |
| | ☐ Inkjet Printer | | |
| | ☐ Photo Printer | | |
| | ☐ Specialty Printer | | |
| | ☐ Portable Printer | | |

FIGURE 4.4—**Home Office Equipment Checklist,** cont.

| Home Office Equipment Type | Make/Model and Notes | Already Have | Need to Purchase |
|---|---|---|---|
| Ring Light for Video Calls and Virtual Meetings | | | |
| Secondary Monitor | | | |
| Smartphone | ☐ Apple iPhone | | |
| | ☐ Android Phone | | |
| | ☐ Other | | |
| Tablet | ☐ iOS (iPad) | | |
| | ☐ Android-Based | | |
| | ☐ Other | | |
| Uninterruptible Power Supply for Your Computer | | | |
| USB Hub | | | |
| Webcam for Video Calls and Virtual Meetings | | | |
| Wifi Router and Signal Extender(s) | | | |
| Other | | | |
| Other | | | |

## The Applications That'll Keep You Productive

The assortment of applications you'll need to get your work done will be determined by what you do for a living, which ones are mandated by your employer, and what tasks you need to accomplish throughout your workday. That said, Figure 4.5 on page 77 offers a selection of popular application categories and examples of specific applications in each category. A wide range of options are available for each.

## SAVE MONEY USING AN INKJET PRINTER WITH INK TANKS

✈ ⋯ ✈

When choosing a printer for your home office, you'll save a lot of money over time if you purchase an all-in-one inkjet printer that relies on ink tanks, as opposed to traditional ink cartridges. Each time you refill the tanks, the ink will last for the equivalent of 20 to 30 individual ink cartridges, for the price of just one cartridge. The initial purchase price of printers that use ink tanks (or toner tanks) is typically about the same as a comparable printer that still uses ink cartridges or toner cartridges, but the long-term savings related to a printer that uses tanks is substantial.

Choose a printer that offers a high-resolution print quality and scanner, along with a fast print speed (measured in pages per minute). You'll also benefit from the printer having at least one paper tray with a capacity of 250 sheets or more. These printers are available from companies like Canon, Epson, HP, and Brother.

If you have a higher printer budget, your home office will benefit from the sharper print quality and higher print speed offered by a color laser printer, but not only are these printers more expensive, but refilling their color toner cartridges is pricey as well. The print yield from each cartridge is also much lower than what you'd get from an ink tank printer.

However, if you don't need to print in color, consider adding an all-in-one monochrome laser printer to your home office setup. You'll benefit from crisper text, a faster print speed, and lower-cost black toner cartridges. These printers, however, do not do a good job with graphics or photographs that were meant to be displayed in full color.

If you must rely on a printer that uses cartridges, look into less expensive "compatible" ink or toner, as opposed to brand-name ink or toner sold by the printer manufacturer. Companies like LD Products (ldproducts.com/) sell compatible ink and toner for virtually all the popular printers on the market.

## SAVE MONEY, CONT.

As for printer paper, save money purchasing cartons of five or ten reams of standard 20-pound copy paper from a local office supply superstore rather than buying one 500-sheet ream at a time. If you'll be using full color and a printer that can handle double-sided printing, however, consider using slightly thicker 24- or 28-pound copy paper to prevent the ink from seeping through each printed page.

FIGURE 4.5—**Remote Worker Application Checklist**

| Application Category | Popular Options | Mandated by Employer or Already Used by Team |
|---|---|---|
| Antivirus/Malware Protection | Bitdefender | |
| | Malwarebytes | |
| | McAfee | |
| | Norton | |
| Bookkeeping | FreshBooks | |
| | NetSuite | |
| | QuickBooks | |
| | Zoho Books | |
| Cloud-Based File Sharing & Remote Storage | Apple iCloud | |
| | Box | |
| | Dropbox | |
| | Google Drive | |
| | Microsoft OneDrive | |
| Contact Management/ Customer Relationship Management (CRM) | Apple Contacts | |
| | HubSpot | |
| | Monday.com CRM | |
| | Netsuite | |
| | Salesforce | |
| | Zoho CRM | |

FIGURE 4.5—**Remote Worker Application Checklist,** cont.

| Application Category | Popular Options | Mandated by Employer or Already Used by Team |
|---|---|---|
| Database | Airtable | |
| | FileMaker | |
| | Microsoft Access | |
| Digital Slide Presentation | Apple Keynote | |
| | Google Slides | |
| | Microsoft PowerPoint | |
| Email Client | Apple Mail | |
| | eM Client | |
| | Gmail | |
| | Mailbird | |
| | Microsoft Outlook | |
| | Spark | |
| | Windows Mail | |
| Expense Tracking | Expensify | |
| | QuickBooks | |
| | Rydoo | |
| | Zoho Expense | |
| File Collaboration | Apple iCloud | |
| | Box | |
| | Dropbox | |
| | Google Drive | |
| | Microsoft OneDrive | |
| Internet Voice Calling (VoIP) | Dialpad | |
| | GoTo Connect | |
| | Grasshopper | |
| | Ooma Office | |
| | RingCentral | |
| | Vonage | |

FIGURE 4.5—**Remote Worker Application Checklist,** cont.

| Application Category | Popular Options | Mandated by Employer or Already Used by Team |
|---|---|---|
| Invoicing/Payment Processing | HoneyBook | |
| | Invoice2go | |
| | PayPal | |
| | Square | |
| | Stripe | |
| | Zoho Invoice | |
| Messaging | Google Chat | |
| | Google Hangouts | |
| | Messenger | |
| | Microsoft Teams | |
| | Skype | |
| | Slack | |
| | Telegram | |
| | WhatsApp | |
| | Zoho Cliq | |
| Note-Taking | Apple Notes | |
| | Evernote | |
| | Google Keep | |
| | Microsoft OneNote | |
| PDF File Reader, Creator, and Editor | Adobe Acrobat | |
| | PDF Expert | |
| Photo Editing | Adobe Express | |
| | Adobe Photoshop | |
| | Apple Photos | |
| | Google Photos | |
| Scheduling/Calendar | Apple Calendar | |
| | Calendly | |
| | Google Calendar | |
| | Microsoft Outlook | |
| | Zoho Calendar | |

FIGURE 4.5—**Remote Worker Application Checklist,** cont.

| Application Category | Popular Options | Mandated by Employer or Already Used by Team |
|---|---|---|
| Spreadsheet | Apple Numbers | |
| | Google Sheets | |
| | Microsoft Excel | |
| Time Tracking | Harvest | |
| | Hours | |
| | HourStack | |
| | Tick | |
| | Timeular | |
| | Toggl Track | |
| To-Do List/Task Manager | Asana | |
| | Google Tasks | |
| | Hive | |
| | Microsoft To Do | |
| | Monday.com | |
| | Trello | |
| Video Calling/Virtual Meeting | Google Meet | |
| | Microsoft Teams | |
| | Skype | |
| | Zoom | |
| Virtual Private Network (VPN) | CyberGhost VPN | |
| | ExpressVPN | |
| | NordVPN | |
| | Norton Secure VPN | |
| | Surfshark | |

FIGURE 4.5—**Remote Worker Application Checklist,** cont.

| Application Category | Popular Options | Mandated by Employer or Already Used by Team |
|---|---|---|
| Web Browser | Apple Safari | |
| | DuckDuckGo | |
| | Firefox | |
| | Google Chrome | |
| | Microsoft Edge | |
| Word Processor | Apple Pages | |
| | Google Docs | |
| | Microsoft Word | |
| | OpenOffice Writer | |
| | WordPerfect | |

In Chapter 6, "How to Remotely Collaborate," we'll focus more on how you can use some of these applications as part of your remote working tool set. However, when choosing specific applications, make sure they're compatible with what your company and team are currently using.

Consider starting with an application suite, such as Microsoft 365 or Google Workspace, that provides a collection of commonly used apps that work seamlessly together, run on all your computers and mobile devices, and offer compatibility with the broadest range of other users (including your co-workers, collaborators, team members, customers, and clients).

## Required Office Supplies

The list of office supplies you'll need will vary greatly. However, here's a general list of common supplies you might want to keep on hand. These items can be purchased online or in person from any office supply superstore.

- Business cards
- Envelopes and packaging supplies
- File folders
- Letterhead
- Markers and highlighters
- Notepads
- Paper clips/binder clips
- Pens/other writing instruments
- Postage stamps
- Printer ink/toner
- Printer paper
- Rubber bands
- Ruler
- Scissors
- Stapler/staples
- Sticky notes
- Tape

## Telephone and Internet Considerations

Several technologies have replaced the traditional landline phone for remote workers. The main one is called Voice over Internet Protocol (VoIP). Basically, this is an app that allows you to make and receive phone calls via the internet, typically for a flat monthly fee. With a VoIP account, you receive a virtual phone number that people can call you on and that will show up on someone's caller ID display when you call them.

With VoIP, you get all the popular features you'd expect from a landline business phone, including caller ID, call forwarding, voicemail, three-way calling, call blocking, call hold, and call waiting. You can also have your own toll-free phone number, call recording, and incoming voice mails automatically transcribed and emailed to you.

Using a single VoIP account, you can make or receive calls from your smartphone, tablet, desktop computer, or laptop via a high-speed internet connection. Depending on your service plan, unlimited calling throughout the United States or to one or all countries is available.

Unlike a messaging service that also offers voice calling, when you use a dedicated VoIP service, the other party does not need to be using that same service. You can call or receive calls from any cellular phone or landline or someone else's VoIP phone line.

When shopping for a VoIP service, here are a few things to consider:

- The selection of calling features offered
- The monthly fee and any additional per-minute charges
- What platforms the VoIP service supports with software or mobile apps

The biggest benefit of using a VoIP service is that you can work from anywhere. Your incoming calls will still ring on the equipment you're using, and you can make outgoing calls from your phone number and the people you're calling won't know where you are. You can be at home, at a remote work location, in a hotel, or at a beach. To achieve the best results, you'll want to invest in good-quality noise-canceling headphones or earbuds with a built-in microphone. While you might get away with using the microphone and speaker built into your smartphone, do not rely on the ones built into your computer or tablet.

There are many VoIP services to choose from. Some of the more popular options among remote workers include:

- *Dialpad*: dialpad.com/
- *GoTo Connect*: goto.com/connect
- *Grasshopper*: grasshopper.com/
- *Ooma Office*: ooma.com/office/
- *RingCentral*: ringcentral.com/
- *Vonage*: vonage.com/

If your smartphone is your primary communications tool, a variety of apps for iPhones and Android-based phones allow you to add a second VoIP phone line to your existing phone. Incoming calls will have a distinctive ringtone so you can keep your personal and business calls separate. Check out the Apple App Store or Google Play Store for apps like Second Phone Number, Second Line 2nd Phone Number, and PhoneLine—2nd Phone Number.

To create and maintain a professional image, especially if you're a small business operator or remote worker who needs to keep up the appearance of working from a traditional office, there are a wide range of virtual assistant companies that will answer incoming calls 24/7 and forward them to you during business hours or take detailed messages during off-hours. This is more costly than using traditional voicemail, but it is a more personalized approach that allows your important customers and clients to speak with another human whenever you're not personally available.

A few of the popular virtual assistant agencies that offer their services in conjunction with VoIP technology include: Posh (posh.com/), Abby Connect (www.abby.com/), and Ruby (ruby.com/). For an independent remote worker or small business, expect to pay between $50 and $100 per month, plus a per-minute fee, to have a live receptionist answer your calls.

## Set Up an Organized Work Space

Once you've gathered all the furniture, equipment, software, and supplies you'll need, the next step is to organize your home office in a manner that's most conducive to your work habits and workflow. Again, you want to ensure that what you need is always at arm's length or very easy to access. Creating a clean and clutter-free work space will help you focus on your work.

If you often print, photocopy, and scan documents while at your desk, having an all-in-one printer setup on your desk or on a printer stand directly next to it makes sense, as does having a trash can at the edge of your desk and a drawer containing your most used office supplies.

Based on your workflow and habits, create a space that makes you comfortable and that's aesthetically pleasing, as well as practical. Unlike a traditional office where there might be rules about how you lay out your office or decorate, those don't apply for a remote office. That said, whenever you participate in a video call or on-camera virtual meeting, make sure whatever is displayed in your background is appropriate. People will pay attention to the books on your bookshelf, artwork that's displayed, or plants that can be seen. While some people choose to blur the background when they're on camera, this might be something you forget to do, so make sure whatever can be caught on camera is work appropriate.

Especially if you're working from a small space, maintaining a clean and organized work space will allow you to be more efficient. You also want to ensure the furniture you choose is functional and ergonomic, as well as placed in a way that's conducive to your workflow.

## Identifying Your Equipment Needs for Working Outside an Office

While millions of people work efficiently and happily from a home office, some remote workers prefer to be able to work from almost anywhere. The equipment needed for this type of remote work is somewhat different, but it also depends largely on what you do for a living.

Let's start with a worksheet that lists commonly used equipment remote workers can use to create a virtual "office" wherever they happen to be—whether it's a hotel room, coffee shop, airport, airplane, shared work space (not operated by their employer), or their vehicle. While you might not need all the equipment listed in Figure 4.6 on page 86, consider what you will need to be able to get your work done and stay in communication while on the go.

## Considerations Before Choosing to Work Outdoors

During many parts of the year (depending on where you live), there are often opportunities for a remote worker to work outdoors: enjoying the sunshine, getting fresh air, but still getting their work done. You could work from your yard, an outdoor café, a local park, a hotel pool, or even a beach.

If you choose to work outside, the equipment listed in Figure 4.5 on page 86 should be your starting point. However, here are four additional things you'll need to think about:

### 1. Cellular Data Internet Connectivity

Unless you're working directly outside your home or in a location with a public wifi hotspot you can connect to, you'll need access to a cellular data network with 4G or 5G connectivity. You can do this with a personal wifi hotspot that you set up via your smartphone. You'll need a cellular

FIGURE 4.6—**Remote Worker Equipment Checklist**

| Remote Office Equipment Type | Make/Model and Notes | Already Have | Need to Purchase |
|---|---|---|---|
| Carry-On Case (with Internal Padded Compartments) to Transport Equipment | | | |
| Laptop Case | | | |
| Laptop Computer | ☐ Windows PC<br>☐ Mac | | |
| Multiport USB Hub | | | |
| Portable Inkjet Printer | | | |
| Portable Monitor (Second Screen for Laptop) | | | |
| Portable Power (Power Bank) | | | |
| Portable Power Strip and Extension Cord (Plus International Power Adapters, If Applicable) | | | |
| Privacy/Antiglare Filter for Laptop Screen | | | |
| Smartphone | ☐ iPhone<br>☐ Android | | |
| Smartphone (Wireless) Charger | | | |
| Tablet/Digital Notepad | ☐ iPad<br>☐ Android | | |
| Wireless Headphones or Earbuds with a Noise-Cancelation Feature | | | |

service plan that includes unlimited data and the ability to create a private wifi hotspot with no data caps. Consult your cellular service provider to determine if your plan already offers this or what it would cost to add it.

Alternatively, purchase a stand-alone personal wifi hotspot device. These devices are battery powered and fit in the palm of your hand. When turned on, they connect to the closest local cellular data network and give you either 4G LTE or 5G connectivity for multiple devices.

Depending on which model you choose, a personal wifi hotspot will work anywhere within the United States or almost anywhere in the world. But you'll need to pay a daily or monthly fee for connectivity or choose a pay-per-gig plan where you pay based on your actual data usage. If you'll only be using the device occasionally, a flat-fee (unlimited) daily plan for around $10 per day is typically the most economical option.

## 2. Glare from the Sun

Working outdoors, the glare from the sun will impact your ability to see your screens. You can either bring along some type of shade for cover or invest in antiglare filters. 3M, for one, offers antiglare and privacy covers that are custom-sized for specific laptop, smartphone, and tablet models.

Of course, you'll also want to protect yourself from the sun's rays by wearing a hat, sunglasses (with UV protection), and sunscreen. Also make sure to apply sunscreen to the backs of your hands, because they'll likely be exposed to the sun while you're typing.

## 3. Noise Issues

When working outdoors, you'll need to deal with the sounds of nature, including birds chirping, dogs barking, and wind. There will also be unwanted noise generated by nearby traffic, airplanes flying overhead, and potentially your neighbors. If you live in the suburbs, the equipment used by landscapers (such as lawn mowers and leaf blowers) can be a constant annoyance.

To overcome these unwanted distractions, invest in a pair of noise-canceling headphones or wireless earbuds. Over-the-ear headphones tend to be more comfortable when worn for extended periods, they often block out unwanted noise a bit better, and their rechargeable battery will last a lot longer (typically at least 20 hours between charges). Make sure they have at least one built-in microphone so you can use them for phone calls, video calls, or virtual meetings.

If you prefer earbuds, they are less cumbersome to carry around, but their battery life is typically much shorter (less than five or six hours if you're using them to block out ambient sounds and make calls).

Apple (apple.com/airpods/), Samsung (bit.ly/3VnyJZ7), Bose (bose.life/3yAIk5l), and OnePlus (www.oneplus.com/) are just a few companies that sell a variety of noise-canceling headphones and earbuds. The Bose QuietComfort 45 or Sony WH-1000XM5 headphones tend to be a favorite among remote workers and frequent travelers due to their comfort, superior noise cancelation, and excellent audio quality.

### 4. Power

Most of your mobile devices are battery powered and offer anywhere from a few hours to more than a day's worth of power between charges. However, if you'll be working remotely for extended periods and won't always have access to an electrical outlet, it makes sense to travel with either a smartphone/tablet external battery pack or a larger and more powerful power bank. A power bank can run your laptop computer as well as your mobile devices for an extended period. However, they tend to be more expensive and they're larger and heavier to carry around.

Some power banks are brick-shaped and weigh between three and five pounds. Others are flat (less than 0.5 inches thick), rectangular, and take up about the same footprint as a laptop computer, making them easier to transport in your laptop case.

As for portable battery packs, these too come in a wide range of sizes and strengths. Some are built into a smartphone case, while others offer a wireless charging pad (so no cables are required to charge the smartphone). Others are about the size of a pack of cigarettes and have multiple charging ports, so you can simultaneously charge your smartphone, tablet, and wireless earbuds.

When it comes to remote power, figure out what devices you will need to keep powered throughout the workday. Then based on your budget, choose the option that offers the strongest battery, with the shortest recharging time, and has the proper charging ports or options for your computer and mobile devices.

Several companies that offer battery packs and power banks include:

- *Anker*: us.anker.com/collections/power-banks
- *Belkin*: belkin.com/us/chargers/c/power-banks/
- *Intelli*: intelli.co/collections/chargers-power-banks

- *MaxOak*: maxoak.net/
- *Mophie*: zagg.com/en_us/mophie

## Don't Just Go on a Massive Shopping Spree

As you start shopping for the equipment and gear you'll rely on as a remote worker, you'll quickly discover there's no shortage of things that promise to make your work easier and help you be more productive. However, before going on a massive shopping spree, focus on your daily work habits and think carefully about where you'll be working from.

Next, when figuring out how you'll pay for everything, consider:

- What equipment you already have
- What your employer (if applicable) will provide
- What you can initially borrow from friends or family
- What can be acquired for free
- What you can purchase used or refurbished

Remember, you can always upgrade your furniture and equipment later or start off with the bare minimum. Then as your budget permits, purchase new furniture, equipment, tools, and applications. Be sure to ask your co-workers or team members what they recommend and pay attention to the ratings and reviews for anything you plan to purchase online.

Remember, too, that technology is constantly evolving. Decide if you require the most current version of that smartphone, tablet, computer, or printer, or if you could potentially save money by purchasing last year's model.

When it comes to software, unless your employer mandates that you use certain applications, look into free or open-source options. Instead of paying for Microsoft 365 (which has all the Office applications), you may be able to use a free office suite that's fully compatible with Microsoft. WPS Office (wps.com/), LibreOffice (libreoffice.org/), OnlyOffice (onlyoffice.com/), or OpenOffice (openoffice.org/) may be viable options. For as little as $6 per user per month, Google Workspace (workspace.google.com) also offers a suite of powerful and popular tools.

Likewise, when it comes to office furniture and lighting, you can take a budget route, find midpriced options, or seek out high-end designs. If you need a folding tripod desk that's extremely portable and can be set up virtually anywhere, a company called Intension Design (intension-design.com/) offers several higher-end, extremely well-made, and highly functional options.

However, if you're on a tight budget, you'll find similar tripod desks (although perhaps of lower quality) at a fraction of the price on Amazon. IKEA (ikea.com/), Overstock (overstock.com/), and Wayfair Professional (wayfair.com/professional/confirm) are also great places to find low-priced and mid-priced office furniture and lighting options.

## CHAPTER 5

# Work Successfully from a Shared Work Space

eing a remote worker means different things to different people. It could mean working from home, a hotel room, a coffee shop, an airport, or anywhere else their life or job takes them. But there's another popular option.

Instead of working from a traditional office operated by their employer, some remote workers choose to work from a shared work space, also commonly referred to as a co-working space. Co-working allows people to work on their own within a traditional office environment that offers a bunch of amenities and services.

*Harvard Business Review* defines co-working as "a membership-based work space where diverse groups of freelancers, remote workers, and other independent professionals work together in a shared, communal setting."

SmallBizGenius.net, a news site for small business owners, reported it's projected that by 2025 there will be around 26,000 shared work space locations available to remote workers worldwide (smallbizgenius.net). As of 2017, the average remote worker using this type of work environment was below the age of 40, and 44 percent of the co-working workforce was female. More than half of the people who opt to work from a co-working location do so for the social aspect and enjoyable atmosphere.

Typically, a shared work space is operated by an independent company and provides a casual office setting for its members. This might mean access to a shared receptionist, a private office, and fully equipped conference rooms. It might also include coffee, snacks, and shared office equipment.

Some shared work spaces offer a communal work environment that encourages its members to interact, socialize, network, and work at large tables or from a cluster of desks. Shared work spaces have become popular in recent years for people who enjoy remote working but don't like the isolation that often comes with it.

Depending on the company, members typically pay a daily, weekly, or monthly fee for access to the facility. They might be charged extra fees for using specific services, equipment, or facilities, such as use of a private conference room (paid for by the hour).

## Benefits of Working from a Shared Work Space

People who use a shared work space tend to love its social aspect, but there are plenty of other benefits as well, including:

- You can work in a casual office setting outside your home.
- It's much more affordable than renting and equipping your own small office.
- Working from a shared work space makes it much easier to separate your home and work life.

··▸ Each shared work space is already equipped with amenities and basic office furniture and equipment, like desks, desk chairs, secure internet access, and printers. Most people simply need to bring their own laptop.

··▸ People working from a shared work space can network and socialize within common areas, greatly reducing the sense of isolation people often experience working from home, or even from a coffee shop. Keep in mind, networking and socializing are two distinct things. Take advantage of both opportunities when appropriate. Socializing means interacting with other people on a personal level, making idle conversation about the weather, sports, personal interests, or your favorite TV show. Networking is socializing with the goal of making work connections (such as finding new customers/clients). With a bit of finesse, you can achieve both in a shared work space.

··▸ In some cases, a support staff (such as a receptionist and IT specialist) is available. Take full advantage of the in-person administrative support at the shared work space, as well as any support that's provided remotely by your employer. Your productivity will improve if you can delegate tasks like photocopying, collating documents, and screening incoming phone calls to someone else.

··▸ Many shared work space providers operate multiple locations, so members can choose which location they want to work from on any given day while also having a place to work from when they travel.

··▸ Basic services like security, restrooms, and cleaning are provided.

··▸ Most shared work spaces are temperature regulated and offer air conditioning, heating, and filtered air circulation.

··▸ When needed, fully equipped conference rooms are available (on a reservation basis) to host meetings.

## 4 Quick Tips for Working from a Shared Work Space

Here are four strategies that'll help you adapt to and perform well while working from any shared work space:

1. Maintain a well-organized and clutter-free desk, especially if it's not yours 24/7. Take advantage of a scanner and cloud-based document

storage service (such as Dropbox) to eliminate as much paper as possible.

2. Even if you have people working directly next to you, create polite but distinct boundaries. Use a "do not disturb" sign if necessary.

3. For your own health and safety, don't just rely on whatever cleaning and sanitizing the shared work space operator provides. Clean up after yourself and disinfect any shared equipment (like photocopiers or printers) before and after you use it.

4. Keep an eye on the time. If you only have access to a shared conference room, office, private phone booth, or other area for a certain amount of time, stick to that schedule to the minute. Also have a contingency plan for important calls or meetings (virtual or in person), if the area you reserved does not become available on time.

## 12 Potential Drawbacks of Working from a Shared Work Space

Depending on the layout and design of the shared work space you select, how much privacy you'll have and the types of distractions you'll encounter on a day-to-day basis will vary greatly. It's important to choose a shared work space with a layout and amenities that match your needs, budget, and desire for social interaction.

While the concept of having a private desk or office in an otherwise bustling environment may sound appealing, think about whether you'll be able to stay focused on your work, or if the temptation to socialize with other people, take constant coffee and snack breaks, or relax in the common lounges or wellness rooms will prevent you from meeting your work responsibilities.

In addition to a wide range of potential distractions, 12 potential drawbacks to a shared work space include:

1. You will be working near potential employers and dealing with a general lack of privacy.

2. You will be unable to fully customize your work space.

3. The shared work space will likely have a different culture than your actual employer.

4. If you're trying to establish a reputable brand for your business, inviting potential customers or clients to a shared work space's conference room for a meeting or presentation could tarnish your brand's image and credibility.

5. Other remote workers who don't follow the facility's rules could create an uncomfortable work environment for everyone else.

6. Some shared work spaces offer an a la carte fee structure, so when you're done paying for all the extras and amenities you require, the overall cost could be much higher than you initially budgeted for.

7. Not all shared work spaces are available to members on a 24/7 basis. Make sure the work space's hours fit your work schedule.

8. Shared conference room access could be limited. In addition to having to reserve a conference room well in advance, based on the occupancy rate of the work space, being able to access a conference room when you need one could become a logistical problem.

9. Not all shared work spaces include (or are close to) ample parking or outside dining options. And the types of office equipment available—such as printers, paper shredders, internet access, photocopiers, and office supplies—vary greatly. Consider your needs carefully.

10. If a shared receptionist and/or office support staff is included, make sure those services will be useful to your type of work, that they will help you enhance or maintain your company's image or reputation, and that the services you need will be available when you need them.

11. Unless the shared work space you choose provides you with your own desk or office, you will not be allowed to alter the design or layout of your space or add any personalized décor.

12. Just as if you were to work from home or another remote location, when working from a shared work space, you will not be closely supervised by your employer. You'll need to become a self-guided worker, capable of motivating yourself, meeting your own deadlines, juggling your own schedule, and being entirely accountable for your output and productivity.

## Tips for Working from a Shared Work Space You Think Meets Your Needs

First, determine exactly what you hope to get out of working from a shared work space. Next, choose a location with the resources, culture, and overall atmosphere where you'll be comfortable working. Then, before signing up for a long-term commitment, try it out for a week or a month.

Once you begin using a shared work space, these guidelines will help you stay productive and focused on your work:

- ⇢ Use noise-canceling headphones to drown out unwanted noise and reduce distractions.

- ⇢ Just as you would when working from home (or anywhere else), create a plan and detailed schedule for each day, complete with a prioritized to-do list. Set realistic expectations, and then plan and prioritize what you need to accomplish.

- ⇢ Take breaks throughout your day, and limit your socializing to before your official workday begins, during scheduled breaks, and after your work hours. Avoid the temptation to wander into shared lounges when you're supposed to be at your desk.

- ⇢ Develop a plan for participating in phone calls, video calls, and virtual meetings that won't distract others while giving you the privacy you'll need.

- ⇢ Determine what office equipment and supplies you'll need and bring along whatever the shared office space does not provide. This might require you to bring your own box of supplies to work each day if you can't securely leave personal items at the location when you're not there.

- ⇢ To get the most out of the social experience offered by a shared work space, participate in the scheduled events that are open to everyone, as long as they don't interfere with your work.

- ⇢ Use digital documents and files, so you have access to everything you'll need without having to rely on file cabinets or lugging large, heavy file boxes to and from the shared work space.

- ⇢ Dress comfortably, but professionally. Because you likely won't be able to customize or control the temperature of the shared work space, wear clothing that won't cause you to be too hot or too cold while you're working.

## Popular Shared Work Space Options

While there are thousands of locally owned shared work spaces around the world, here are a few of the national and international companies that operate hundreds of locations.

### *Discover WeWork Shared Work Spaces*

In March 2022, Apple TV+ began streaming an original series called *WeCrashed*, starring Jared Leto and Anne Hathaway. It delved into the history of WeWork, one of the world's largest and most successful shared work space providers, which was founded in 2010.

Despite the company's tumultuous early days, the now stable and well-operated business currently operates more than eight hundred locations worldwide—providing shared work spaces when and where remote workers need them. These days, whether you choose a month-to-month or long-term membership option, a typical WeWork location offers its members multiple options, including:

- A dedicated desk in a shared office with shared amenities
- A private and lockable small office space
- A fully furnished private office suite with amenities
- A full-floor office, which is an entire private floor of an office building from which a business can operate
- Available indoor and outdoor event and production spaces

Depending on the WeWork location, shared amenities include enhanced cleaning and disinfecting services throughout the day, conference rooms, on-site staff, and the use of common areas. What the company calls "phone booths" are available for participating in private calls. Many locations also host scheduled networking events, and all provide hardwired Ethernet or secure wifi internet connectivity and access to printers, basic office supplies, and a paper shredder.

The cost will depend on the type of work space you need and the membership level you opt for. That said, for someone wanting to work in Boston, Massachusetts, the cost of a WeWork All Access pass (which provides a dedicated desk in a shared office space, shared amenities, five credits per month for meeting room bookings, and 120 black-and-white and 20 color page prints per month) runs around $300 per month as of mid-2022. The company offers a 25 percent discount for the first three months. A dedicated desk means the same desk is yours 24/7 for as long as you're a member. Thus, you have the ability to lock your belongings in your desk drawers. Some locations of WeWork (and other shared work spaces) alternatively provide desk space, but you don't always get the same desk. At the end of the day, you're expected to pack up all your belongings and take them with you—leaving the desk clean and empty.

In addition to monthly plans, there's a pay-as-you-go option for remote workers, allowing people to use facilities and shared amenities at a specific location while paying by the day or even by the hour. The monthly membership, however, is much more affordable than renting a small private office and allows you to interact with other remote workers. For more information about WeWork, visit wework.com/.

### Industrious Offers 120-Plus Locations Across the U.S. and Abroad

Industrious is another option for remote workers that includes a wide range of amenities, from access to private conference rooms to secure wifi, unlimited color printing, office supplies, daily breakfasts, and snacks. Some locations are also dog friendly.

Instead of offering a shared common work space, Industrious provides private offices and office suites with shared common spaces, meeting rooms, wellness rooms, and lounges. The benefit of this arrangement is increased privacy and greater ability to focus on your work without distractions from others. While members have 24/7 access to the facilities, each location is staffed by one or more community managers and operations associates on weekdays, between 8 A.M. and 5 P.M.

Membership fees are based on the location but are available on a month-to-month or long-term basis. All offices come fully furnished with oak desks and Herman Miller office chairs, but members can also bring their own office furniture and décor. Unlike other shared office space options, Industrious offers truly all-inclusive membership plans, with no additional fees. For more information about Industrious shared office spaces, visit industriousoffice.com/.

## Chances Are You'll Find Regus Shared Work Spaces Close to You

As of 2022, Regus had more than 2.5 million customers worldwide in the fast-growing co-working business category, offering thousands of locations around the world. Regus features a variety of shared work space options, including furnished private offices that are ready to move into and offices that are custom-tailored to meet your needs. In addition, the company offers an office membership that gives you access to a private office by the day or for a predetermined number of days per month.

You can even take advantage of offices that are available on an hourly basis. The company's private offices include access to shared lounges, breakout areas, and conference rooms, and a nice selection of amenities, including business-grade wifi, access to printers and scanners, a professional reception team, administrative services, and the ability to find and reserve office space at any location via the Regus app. Access to just the lounges (along with the wifi, printers, scanners, and photocopiers) at any location starts at less than $100 per month.

Meanwhile, the ability to work from a private office and take advantage of receptionist services and lounges starts at just over $100 per month (for a five-day-per-month pass) and goes up to $500-plus per month for the company's office membership. This gives you daily access to an office along with the services and amenities all other plans offer. For more information about Regus shared office spaces, visit regus.com/en-us.

## Choose from More Than 80 Office Evolution Co-Working Locations

For people interested in a co-working environment, Office Evolution offers shared work spaces. Rates start as little as $100 per month, although you'll pay extra for individual services and some amenities, such as the use of meeting rooms or the ability to use their mailing address as your company's business address. If you need more than just a desk, chair, and internet access, Office Evolution also offers access to a private office.

As of mid-2022, Office Evolution was operating more than 80 co-working spaces nationwide and had plans to open up to 140 locations in the U.S. Each location offers a variety of membership plans that can include access to a shared work space, a dedicated desk (with a locking cabinet), a private office, or a smaller, private "micro office." For more information about Office Evolution, visit officeevolution.com/.

## There Are Many More Shared Work Space Options to Choose From

With the mandate to provide flexibility and affordability and increase productivity, while furnishing a work setting that offers networking and socializing opportunities, WeWork, Industrious, Regus, and Office Evolution are just a few of the larger nationwide (or in some cases global) providers of co-working spaces. To find additional options in your city or state (or wherever you need to work from), enter the phrase "local shared work spaces" or "local co-working spaces" into your favorite search engine.

Now that you have a general idea of what you can expect from this type of work environment, decide what exactly you're looking for, how often you'll need the work space, and what amenities and services will be beneficial. Then depending on your budget, choose the option that best matches your work habits.

In addition to the information you find online, almost all shared work spaces will provide free tours and one-day guest passes so you can try working from their location for at least a day before signing up for a membership plan.

### *No Matter Where You Work From, You Need to Become an Effective Collaborator*

Most people who work remotely still need to work with other people— directly or indirectly. However, since each of your collaborators will likely be working from different locations, how you communicate and get your work done will likely be very different compared with working together from a traditional office. The focus of the next chapter is on how to collaborate effectively when working remotely.

## CHAPTER 6

# How to Remotely Collaborate

One of the things you'll most likely need to continue doing while working remotely is working in conjunction with your co-workers or team. This means maintaining the lines of communication, sharing content, and collaborating on specific projects or tasks with people working from different locations.

This chapter focuses on collaborating on tasks and projects with your co-workers and teammates. There are two main types of remote collaboration. The first involves individual co-workers handling their responsibilities on a project on their own. Ultimately the project comes together because everyone works independently to handle their pieces of it, while the project manager works to coordinate and piece it together.

The second way remote workers collaborate is in real time, using online tools. This means that members of a team or co-workers go online at the same time, from their respective remote locations, and use the same tool(s) simultaneously. Several people can work at once on the same Microsoft Word document, Excel spreadsheet, or PowerPoint presentation using the real-time collaboration tools built into Microsoft 365.

Collaboration typically requires an efficient way to communicate (by voice call, video call, virtual meeting, IM, text messaging, or email). You'll also need a way to share data via the cloud (using a file sharing service or tool). For collaborating in real time, you and everyone you're working with will also need access to the same application.

There are some single collaboration tools, like Slack, that allow teams to handle many of these tasks and offer seamless integration with hundreds of other applications. There are also plenty of software suites that include multiple applications designed to work seamlessly together and that have collaboration tools built in. Microsoft 365 (microsoft.com/en-us/microsoft-365/business) and Google Workspace (workspace.google.com/business) are examples of this. Countless project management, CRM, and other types of applications also now accommodate team members and collaborators working remotely.

In fact, to keep up with the increase in the remote workforce since the start of COVID-19, just about every major application that's used for any type of work-related task has been (and continues to be) updated with new functionality designed to accommodate remote workers.

## 10 Tips for Collaborating Using Online Tools

Here are 10 strategies to help you better collaborate online:

1. Kick off a conversation, meeting, or collaboration session with some informal pleasantries. Not only will this help everyone change their focus from their previous work to the current task, but it'll also foster more personal relationships across the team.

2. With roughly 65 percent of the general population being "visual learners," it makes sense to use visuals when brainstorming, interacting, or communicating online with co-workers and teammates. Take advantage of colorful pictures, charts, and graphs, and use an interactive whiteboard to help get important points across—as opposed to just using text and numbers.

3. While there are plenty of tools that allow people to interact via IM and file sharing, sometimes it makes sense to also participate in a short video call or virtual meeting (5 to 15 minutes long) to communicate important information, clarify a miscommunication, correct an error, or ensure everyone on the team understands the topic or issue.

4. When working on a specific project with one person or a group of people, try to keep all communication and content in one place—not scattered across multiple applications or files.

5. Make sure all the most up-to-date information for a project is available to all pertinent people on your team. If they have to search for timely information or rely on old versions of files, it wastes time and puts the whole team at a disadvantage.

6. Pay attention to the clock. When setting up a time to collaborate with others, schedule a specific time (15, 30, or 60 minutes), and then stick to that schedule. Avoid long collaboration sessions, and don't go over the allocated time, because people will likely have other important meetings or tasks on their schedule. You can always schedule a second session later, if needed. If you do go longer than one hour, be sure to give everyone a five- to ten-minute break during the session to avoid fatigue.

7. Nominate a team leader. No matter how small, every project or task that involves two or more people collaborating should have a team leader to keep everything (and everyone) organized and on track.

8. Ensure all team members are held accountable. It's very easy for team members to sit back and let others do the work. This is referred to as "social loafing," and it's a problem when dealing with less productive teammates or co-workers. By assigning everyone

very specific tasks and deadlines and communicating clear expectations, it's easier to hold everyone accountable for getting their work done.

9. Follow an organized and structured approach, with defined expectations and realistic deadlines. When collaborating on a larger project, gather the team together at the start and develop an organized approach to completing your tasks. Set realistic expectations and deadlines, and be sure to outline any procedures that need to be precisely followed. Discuss everything in a virtual meeting and then follow up in writing, so there are no misunderstandings and people have a resource they can refer to when they have questions.

10. Create detailed profiles within all communication and collaboration tools. Chances are, as a remote worker, you'll need to communicate with dozens or even hundreds of different people using various online tools. When collaborating with a group, make sure everyone creates a detailed profile for themselves within each collaboration tool. This profile should include their full name, job title, a headshot, and a brief description (one or two sentences) of their job responsibilities. These profiles make it easier to remember names, understand the hierarchy within a team or organization, and quickly determine whom to contact when specific questions or problems arise.

## Pinpoint and Gather the Collaboration Tools You Need

Back in Chapter 4, "How to Set Up and Organize Your Home or Remote Office," we gave you a list of application categories, along with specific and commonly used applications in each of them. Now let's focus more on choosing the right collection of applications for communicating and collaborating. Again, depending on what you do for work, who you work for, and your employment status, you may wind up being told exactly which applications to use and how to use them. However, there are many situations in which you may need to work with different sets of applications when working for different customers or clients, or you may discover that different divisions or groups within a company follow different sets of guidelines. Even if you're told specifically which applications to use for specific tasks, as a remote worker, you want to become familiar with what other options are available. And if you're a freelancer, an independent small business operator, or a department head, you might become the decision-maker regarding which applications you and your team use.

With so many computer and mobile applications now designed to integrate with each other and accommodate remote workers and teams working from many different locations, the key is for each company or team to select the most appropriate tools for their workflow and then make sure that all employees (including remote workers) have secure access to those applications from their respective Windows PCs, Macs, iOS mobile devices, and Android-based mobile devices. Cross-platform compatibility is essential. This becomes much easier when the applications being used are primarily cloud-based.

Depending on what types of communication and collaboration you'll need to do on an ongoing basis, consider the types of functionalities you'll need for yourself and your entire team—making sure that everyone is using the same applications for the same purposes.

The following is a selection of the common collaboration tasks most remote workers need to perform. Of course, what you do for a living will have a huge impact on the tools you actually need and will be relying on moving forward.

## Messaging

Just as your smartphone can send and receive text messages (via its cellular network) as well as IM (via internet messaging services), your computer can also send and receive IM using a variety of services. A message typically consists of text and can also include graphics and file attachments such as photos. Once it is sent, the recipient can view the message almost instantly. They can then respond immediately or whenever it is convenient.

Most IM services allow for one-on-one or group messaging. They are cloud-based, but they offer apps for Windows PCs, Macs, and all mobile devices—allowing users to communicate from whichever device they're currently using.

Once you and your team determine that IM will be an important part of your overall communication strategy, you'll need to choose one specific messaging service, have everyone set up an account with that service, and then have them set up the service to work on each of their computers and mobile devices.

Next, you'll need to establish company or team policies or etiquette for using the messaging service. Set guidelines for when it's appropriate to send messages to co-workers or teammates, whether a business or more casual tone is appropriate, and what types of topics are acceptable in messages.

In addition to one-on-one messaging, most IM tools allow you to create specific channels or chat groups that are great for teams to discuss specific topics. Smaller groups can also communicate in group chats, while two people can communicate directly using one-on-one chats. While these services are available 24/7 for unlimited messaging, most people will be annoyed at receiving messages after work hours, on holidays, or on weekends. Unless there's a legitimate emergency, set policies dictating the hours during which co-workers can message one another, and spell out exactly what constitutes a "work emergency." That said, when used appropriately, an IM service provides a low-cost, highly efficient, and versatile way for remote workers to communicate.

## Project Management

The necessary components of any project management tool are customizability, flexibility, and the ability to accommodate remote team members. Basically, a project management application is designed to:

- Help an organization or team organize project tasks, responsibilities, and budget
- Easily handle related scheduling in a way that's accessible and clear to everyone involved
- Allow the project manager or leader to assign roles and responsibilities, track progress, and keep the entire team on track to meet deadlines
- Easily organize and display deadlines, milestones, and goals using text, charts, and graphics
- Handle the five main stages of project management (conception, planning, execution, performance monitoring, and project completion)

while also dealing with things like resource planning, risk identi-
fication, scheduling, communication, quality control, and budget
management

The best project management applications are designed to improve
communication, offer flexibility, be collaborative, and integrate with other
popular business applications.

## Email

While not everyone needs to use the same email client to manage
their work email account, they should all offer the same functionality
and tools for sending, receiving, organizing, and managing all email
communications in a way that meets the company's policies and
security protocols. Because some email clients also integrate seamlessly
with group scheduling applications (like Microsoft Outlook), if this is
something a company or team will be using, it makes sense for everyone
to use the same email client.

## Virtual Meetings and Video Calls

Everyone has probably heard of (and come to rely on) services like Zoom or
Microsoft Teams to handle videoconferencing and virtual meetings. These
applications and similar ones are commonly used in almost every industry,
and not just among remote workers. While each of these virtual meeting
tools offers the same core functionality, each has a unique collection of
features and security measures. They all are also typically accessible from
any type of computer or mobile device. However, to participate in a video
call, videoconference, or virtual meeting, all the attendees must use the
same service.

It makes sense for each team or organization to choose one videocon-
ferencing/virtual meeting platform. However, as a remote worker, you'll
likely need to become proficient in and have access to multiple services,
since customers, clients, and people outside your team or organization
may use other services.

Once you know which service you'll be using, install the proper application on each of your computers and mobile devices, become proficient

in its use, and keep it updated with the latest version, because all these services are constantly evolving.

Within your organization or team, you'll also want to establish rules for using this type of app so everyone can communicate as efficiently as possible, regardless of where they're working from.

### Document and Content Collaboration

Whether you're using Google Docs, Microsoft Word, or another word processor, these applications allow you to collaborate in real time with one or more people and easily share documents via the cloud so multiple people can make changes to them on their own time. This functionality is built into all applications in the Google Workspace and Microsoft 365 suites, as well as countless other applications.

When using any of these collaboration tools, the file creator needs to be very careful when sharing or inviting other people to access it. You could invite people to view a document you have created, but not allow them to edit it, save it to their computers, or print it. Alternatively, you can provide someone else with full access and permissions to alter and share that document as they deem necessary.

The file creator can also add password protection to a file, so even if the wrong person gets access to it, they can't open it without knowing the password. As members of a team change, the file creator may need to periodically update, add, or revoke permissions for individual files. For all the applications you'll be using for collaboration, learn to use the file sharing and real-time collaboration tools. This will not only save you time, but it'll also help reduce human error and data breaches resulting from file sharing and permissions setting mistakes.

### File Sharing

When it comes to sharing files with others, compatibility is a key issue. Make sure that the people you'll be sharing a specific file or folder with have the application or tool needed to open, view, and work with it. As stated above, take steps to avoid human error associated with sharing the wrong files/folders with the wrong people or granting inappropriate permissions to specific people.

Cloud-based file sharing tools, like Dropbox, Microsoft OneDrive, and Google Drive, make it easy to store files in the cloud and provide others with limited or full access to them. However, one person should be in charge of managing those files: setting permissions, creating descriptive file names that everyone will be able to identify, and organizing them within well-labeled folders and subfolders that provide an easy-to-understand file storage system.

While still taking all necessary security precautions, the easier it is for the appropriate people to find, access, and use the files and content they need, the more productive everyone on the team or within the organization will be.

## CRM Application

Customer relationship management (CRM) applications are basically interactive databases designed for members of an organization to maintain detailed records about customers and clients, so any member of a team can quickly see an overview of a specific customer or client, what communications or interactions they've had with your organization, and what needs to be handled moving forward. A CRM application is customizable and tracks most or all of the interactions a company has with the people it does business with.

For a CRM application to function well within an organization, it is essential for the company to choose the most appropriate application (and there are many to choose from)—but it's also vital for all employees who will be using it to adhere to the same procedures for creating records and keeping them up-to-date.

Salesforce is one of the most widely used CRM applications across many different industries and by organizations of all sizes. Visit salesforce.com/crm/what-is-crm/ to learn more.

An organization can benefit from using a CRM application in many ways. It provides a snapshot of each customer or client that can be used for cross-functional insight and reporting. It also makes it easy to quickly gather current information about a customer, client, or supplier, so you can provide proactive service. Most important, CRM applications offer simplified (and in some cases automated) tools for real-time collaboration when it comes to collecting, sharing, and accessing important client-specific data.

Ultimately, the goal of a CRM application is to give a company the tools to provide exceptional customer service to their clients or customers, and at the same time, maintain detailed records that all relevant people within an organization have real-time access to. As a remote worker, a CRM application gives you cloud-based access to data that is continuously updated by your co-workers and team members, so regardless of where you're working from, you'll always have up-to-date information at your fingertips.

According to the Salesforce website (salesforce.com/crm/benefits-of-crm/), "All team members can gather insights and data and work together to provide exceptional customer-centric experiences. Data organized and presented by a CRM platform leads to a better understanding of customers. This leads to better messaging and outreach, much of which can be done with automation, which helps you offer better, more efficient customer service. Furthermore, your teams can collaborate more easily. Of all the benefits of CRM software, using data and technology to power a more efficient company is one of the biggest. This helps you manage customer relationships more effectively, leading to better business."

## Virtual Whiteboards

Just about every traditional office conference room contains a whiteboard with colorful and erasable markers. The whiteboard can be used for note-taking, brainstorming, and sharing important information during in-person meetings. However, now that more people are working remotely, the physical whiteboard has gone virtual.

Just about every popular virtual meeting, cloud-based file sharing, and real-time collaboration application now offers a virtual whiteboard feature that allows people to use their mouse or a stylus (if they're using a device with a touchscreen) to write or draw while interacting with others online.

Virtual whiteboards can be used in the same way as traditional whiteboards. However, because people are working remotely and everyone has access to virtual markers, it makes sense to set up guidelines about when

## 10 STRATEGIES FOR USING A VIRTUAL WHITEBOARD

Whiteboards are great for visual thinking and for presenting information in real time. Any time you're using a virtual whiteboard during a one-on-one collaboration session or during a virtual meeting, consider these 10 basic strategies:

1. Choose the most appropriate whiteboarding tool for the functionality you and your team need. If the virtual meeting or collaboration tool you already use does not offer whiteboarding, Google "collaborative whiteboard" or "virtual whiteboard" to find free or low-cost alternatives that are cloud-based, secure, and compatible with everyone's computer or mobile devices.

2. Start by defining how the whiteboard will be used during the virtual meeting.

3. Begin each meeting with a blank whiteboard.

4. Consider using a whiteboarding template to help you format your content in a more organized and professional way. There are many available templates suitable for brainstorming sessions, strategy planning, project management, and product development.

5. Develop a system for collaboration, so only one person is writing or drawing on the whiteboard at once, such as when they're presenting or sharing an idea.

6. Unlike a traditional whiteboard, a virtual whiteboard's size is limitless. You get an infinite canvas. That's why it's important to keep the information well-organized. Set aside specific areas of the virtual whiteboard for different types of information, based on established categories or topic headings.

7. Consider adopting a standardized color-coding system. At a glance, people should know the visual meaning of what's created in each specific color.

8. Set a time limit for each meeting or brainstorming session and put someone in charge to keep the collaboration focused, so it doesn't go off on random or unrelated tangents.

**10 STRATEGIES,** CONT.

9. If the application allows for it, consider recording your whiteboarding sessions so you can play back everything that was said while you're viewing the content on the whiteboard.

10. Once an online collaboration using a whiteboard ends, make sure all participants have access to the digital file.

you should contribute and when you should simply view what's being displayed on the whiteboard.

Once basic guidelines are established, a virtual whiteboard is a colorful way for people to share information. Content created on a virtual whiteboard can be saved in any of several popular file formats, including PDF; shared; printed; and managed like any other file.

## Determine How Each Application Will Be Used and Establish Etiquette

After you and your team or organization decide which collaboration tools you will be using, set aside time to establish the protocols and etiquette co-workers should adhere to when using each tool. Put it all in writing in a document that can be continuously updated as needed.

Again, to get the most out of any online collaboration tool, everyone needs to be using the same version of the same tool. File compatibility is also essential, and everyone needs to understand how, when, and for what the tool should be used. Everyone must become proficient at using the selected tools and understand the security procedures they need to follow to prevent unauthorized access or human error that could lead to a data breach or other costly and time-consuming mistakes.

According to a 2020 article published by the *Harvard Business Review* (hbr.org/2020/10/4-tips-for-effective-virtual-collaboration), "Team collaboration done right is a powerful force to align a group of individuals to accomplish a common goal in the most effective way possible. But even the best collaborations, filled with smart, capable, and experienced team members, can be a struggle. Done wrong, collaborative projects can feel like a waste of time where individuals spend more time *talking* about doing things than actually getting things done."

To get everyone on the same page when it comes to online collaboration, consider having all team members participate in a free or low-cost online course that focuses on teaching basic online collaboration skills. Essentials of Team Collaboration, for example, is an online class under an hour in length, offered by LinkedIn Learning (bit.ly/3MqyLeR).

## Strategies for Dealing with Time Zone Scheduling Issues

Any time you're collaborating with other people and dealing with a time zone difference, live collaboration sessions are often more difficult to schedule. Scheduling concessions will need to be made, and some people might even need to work before or after their normal business hours. It's important to set boundaries and schedules, so nobody is consistently expected to participate in a daily or weekly live virtual meeting at 3 A.M.

When working across multiple time zones, a team will need to rely more on asynchronous communications that do not require an immediate response. For this method of collaboration to work seamlessly, you will need to establish effective systems, processes, and protocols. Plus, collaborators need to communicate efficiently through IM and email to compensate for the lack of live interactions.

When you or your teammates know you'll be working from a different time zone, it's important for each person to post in their profile (on each communication and collaboration tool) which time zone they're working from and take advantage of the "Away" status the online collaboration tools offer. This will prevent messages from setting off alerts, alarms, or other notifications outside their normal work hours.

If you know a co-worker is 3, 6, or even 12 hours ahead of (or behind) your time zone, it's important to plan ahead, especially if you have an upcoming deadline and will need their feedback or input. If you have a report due on Monday morning (New York time) but need feedback from

## TAKE ADVANTAGE OF A TIME ZONE MANAGEMENT TOOL

While Google Calendar, Microsoft Outlook, and Apple Calendar allow you to create events and enter appointments based on a specific time zone (and will adjust local time accordingly), there are other world clock and scheduling apps that make working with people across multiple time zones much easier.

The free timeanddate.com website (timeanddate.com/) makes it easy to calculate the difference between time zones, including daylight-saving time (when applicable).

If you're working with a team, Timezone.io (timezone.io) allows you to display each co-worker's name, photo, time zone, and local time on a single screen. With this service, you can see what time it is at everyone's location in a quick glance.

Other online world clock applications and scheduling tools to help you keep track of where (and when) your co-workers are working include TimeTemperature.com (timetemperature.com/) and 24timezones (24timezones.com/#/map).

There are also countless free and low-cost apps available for iOS and Android mobile devices designed to help keep track of multiple time zones at once. For example, all iPhones and iPads have the World Clock app preinstalled, while all Android devices have the Clock app preinstalled. There's also the World Clock Widgets app, World Clock-Local Time app, Time Buddy app, and World Clock Live app, for example, that are available from the Apple App Store or Google Play Store.

co-workers in Japan (which is 14 hours ahead of New York standard time), you'll need to connect with the people in Japan early on Thursday (your time), so they can respond by Friday (their time), allowing you to complete the report in time to submit it on Monday.

Within messages, emails, and other correspondence between team members working from different time zones, it's essential that everyone spell out deadlines and dates in a standardized format, such as "Friday, July 7, 2023, at 2:30 P.M. EST." Include the time zone and refrain from more abstract language, such as "by end of day today" or "before lunchtime," as this will mean something very different to people working in time zones that are one, three, five, or more hours apart.

Ideally, when working with a team that's spread across multiple time zones, try to schedule a few hours of "overlap time" in the working day at a somewhat convenient time for everyone, so that live video calls, virtual meetings, phone calls, or IM are possible.

Especially when team members or co-workers are traveling, it's often hard to keep track of the time zone everyone is in. Be patient and understanding when people make mathematical errors trying to figure out time zone differences.

## CHAPTER 7

# Working with PDF Files Instead of Paper Files

Portable document format (PDF) is an industry-standard file format developed in 1992. It's accessible and viewable from almost any computer or mobile device, which is what makes it so useful in the workplace. When using PDF files, there are no compatibility issues between Windows PCs and Macs, and the same document can be viewed or managed from an iPhone, iPad, or Android phone or tablet.

According to Adobe, "It's a versatile file format created by Adobe that gives people an easy, reliable way to present and exchange documents—regardless of the software, hardware, or operating systems being used by anyone who views the document. It's now an open standard, maintained by the International Organization for Standardization (ISO)."

When a document gets exported into the PDF format, its formatting (including all its fonts, typestyles, colors, and layout) gets saved exactly how it appears in the original. That formatting will remain identical and intact no matter what computer or device it's then imported into or what size screen or monitor it's being viewed on.

## Work with PDF Files from Any Computer or Mobile Device

Because this is an industry-standard file format, your computer or mobile device already has an application installed that allows you to view these documents. For example, on a Mac, iPhone, or iPad, it's the Preview app. But there are also countless free PDF readers for your computers and mobile devices that allow you to view, store, and print these files. Adobe Acrobat Reader (adobe.com/acrobat/pdf-reader.html) is by far the most popular. It's available for free for Windows PCs and Macs.

However, if you want to create, edit, annotate, or have full creative control over your PDFs, you'll need a more robust application, such as Adobe Acrobat Pro, PDF Expert, or any one of countless other applications, which you will need to either purchase outright or pay a monthly subscription fee to use.

That said, many applications you likely already use, such as your favorite web browser and all Microsoft 365 applications (including Word, Excel, PowerPoint, and Outlook) allow you to export the files you're working with into PDFs. This is also true for Google applications like Google Docs and Google Sheets.

Visit adobe.com/documentcloud/integrations.html to learn more about how PDF file compatibility has been fully integrated into hundreds of other popular applications used by remote workers. Oracle NetSuite, Zoho, Salesforce, Dropbox, Box, and countless others all offer PDF file integration and compatibility.

The easiest way to transform a paper document into a file that can be shared electronically—if you need it to retain its formatting—is to turn it into a PDF. All your paper files (including contracts, correspondence, receipts, forms, brochures, reports, etc.) can easily be scanned and saved as PDFs (using a scanner connected to your computer or the camera in your mobile device). These files can then be stored locally or in the cloud.

Maintaining PDF files of all your important documents will allow you to greatly reduce paper clutter, eliminate or greatly diminish the need for file cabinets in your remote work space, and help ensure that the documents you need are always accessible to you. Whether you're working from your home office, a coffee shop, a hotel room, or even an airplane, if you need an important document that's been stored in the cloud, it's only a few keystrokes or on-screen taps away.

PDFs have also become far more versatile in terms of what content can be exported into a PDF and what can be done with those files after they've been created. With the right software, a PDF can be digitally signed, tracked, annotated, edited, printed, stored, password protected, encrypted, and shared in a variety of ways. You can save a form as a PDF that can then be completed by someone else and stored or shared. They can also include text, graphics, images, and all sorts of other content in the form of embedded attachments. An embedded attachment is a file that's attached to a PDF file that will open within a separate app when you click on it.

Regardless of what type of work you do, you'll likely be receiving, working with, and sharing PDFs on a regular basis. Thus, beyond just having the ability to view these files, you'll also want at least one application that allows you to create, edit, annotate, sign, print, manage, store, and share these files. In fact, the application you use to work with PDFs may become as essential to your workflow as your email client and web browser.

Suppose you're working from a coffee shop, and an important client sends you a contract via email that you must review and sign immediately. If the file is a Word document, with the proper software, you could review and annotate the contract as needed, export it into a PDF, and then insert a digital replica of your handwritten signature, while also initialing the paragraphs or pages that require it. Depending on what PDF management application you use, you can then track the signatures and keep tabs on who's seen, reviewed, and signed the document as it gets passed around via email. If the file is already in the PDF format, however, there are tools that allow you to sign that document and return it with a few clicks or on-screen taps. DocuSign (docusign.com) is a tool that works with PDF files that makes it easy to send, receive, review, and sign PDF documents in a highly secure way.

## Why PDFs Are Replacing Traditional Paperwork

There are many reasons PDFs have become so widely used as a replacement for paper documents—especially among remote workers. Some of the most compelling advantages of PDFs are that they're:

- *Colorful.* You're not limited to black-and-white text. All the colors in your original document (including the fonts, photos, charts, and other graphics) will remain, regardless of how or where the file is being viewed.
- *Compact.* The file size of a PDF is relatively small, so they take up little storage space. This also makes them easy and quick to upload/download or send via text or IM. If a large PDF file is created (due to the size of the original document), file compression utilities can reduce its size without compromising readability.
- *Interactive.* A PDF can include links to websites or specific locations within a long document. You can also associate file attachments and all sorts of other content (music, videos, comments or annotations, graphics, and photos) within a PDF. Adobe reports, "PDF docs can contain links, buttons, form fields, audio, video, and business logic. They can be signed electronically and can easily be viewed."
- *Portable.* Any computer or mobile device can use a free application to view any PDF.
- *Recognized Worldwide.* Users from around the world on virtually any operating system, internet browser, or mobile device experience zero compatibility issues with PDFs. And thanks to email, you can send them anywhere in the world in a matter of seconds.
- *Searchable.* Using the search tool built into a PDF reader, you can look for any keyword or phrase. You can also create links within a

PDF, so the reader can click or tap on an interactive table of contents to jump between sections or chapters.

- *Secure.* When you create a PDF, you can add password protection and encryption. This makes it much harder for unauthorized people to open and read the file, even if they get their hands on it. PDFs can also be created as view only, so they cannot be printed, stored locally, or shared by the person viewing them. When these security tools are used, PDFs meet ISO 32000 standards for electronic document exchange.
- *Trackable.* With the right application, the creator of a PDF can keep track of who sees it, what they do with it, and when they access it. The viewing history is time and date stamped, and not editable.
- *Viewable.* Again, once created, a PDF's appearance and formatting remain intact, no matter what type of computer or mobile device you're using to view it. PDFs are also easily formatted to meet a range of accessibility standards, so people with disabilities can more readily use their content.

## A PDF Reader Is a Must

Just about every computer and mobile device comes with a PDF file viewer preinstalled. But many of these apps offer very limited functionality beyond simply reading PDFs. Part of your toolbox should be an application that allows you to work with these files as a practical alternative to paperwork.

### Adobe Acrobat Reader vs. Acrobat Pro

Adobe Acrobat Reader (adobe.com/acrobat/pdf-reader.html) is a free PDF viewer application available for Windows PCs, Macs, iPhones, iPads, and Android-based devices. However, its functionality is limited to allowing you to view, add comments to, and print PDF files, unless you pay a monthly subscription fee.

If you also want to be able to edit files; scan documents and save them as PDF files; sign, track, and send those files; or convert PDFs into file types that can be edited in applications such as Microsoft Word, Excel, or PowerPoint, you'll need to upgrade to Adobe Acrobat Pro DC.

This application is available via a subscription that costs between $12.99 and $24.99 per month (as of mid-2022).

For individual users, the more expensive version of Acrobat Pro (adobe.com/acrobat.html) also allows you to compare two versions of a PDF and spot their differences. Plus, you can transform scanned documents into editable and searchable PDFs, redact or permanently remove content from PDFs, and adjust them to meet ISO and accessibility standards.

Because these applications are continuously being updated with new features, to compare the various versions of Acrobat Reader and Acrobat Pro, visit adobe.com/acrobat/pricing/compare-versions.html, but keep in mind, you have other options.

While the Preview app that comes preinstalled on all Macs allows you to view PDFs, a separate application called PDF Expert (pdfexpert.com) from Readdle is available for the Mac, iPhone, and iPad. It offers a comprehensive suite of tools for creating, viewing, editing, annotating, working with, and managing PDFs. This application can be purchased outright and has no monthly fees associated with it. A monthly subscription plan for PDF Expert is also available, starting at $6.67 per user, per month (as of mid-2022).

For Windows PCs, many applications to handle PDFs are also available. Some of these include:

- *Foxit PDF Editor*: foxit.com/pdf-editor/
- *Nitro PDF Pro*: gonitro.com/pdf-pro
- *PDF Architect*: pdfforge.org/pdfarchitect
- *PDF-XChange Editor*: bit.ly/3EBSx5h
- *Wondershare PDFelement*: pdf.wondershare.com

## Easy Ways to Create PDF Files

From many apps that run on a Windows PC or Mac, there are at least two standard ways to export your document into a PDF. The first is to select the application's Print command. Then, instead of choosing a printer, select the PDF option. The second way is to choose the application's Save As command. Then, when selecting the file format, choose PDF. However, if the app you're working with does not allow you to create a PDF with either of these methods, chances are there's a separate app or online utility that can help you out. Adobe Acrobat Pro DC or PDF Expert are two examples. There are also versions of these and other apps that work with iOS and Android-based mobile devices (and will automatically sync documents and files with your computers).

From a computer, if you want to create a PDF from a paper document, you'll need to connect an optical scanner to the computer and then use the software that comes with the scanner to save the scanned document as a PDF. However, other applications listed in the previous section also support scanning functionality, meaning they can take control over your scanner and create PDF files from scanned documents directly.

There are many different types of scanners. Some are designed for a specific purpose, like scanning receipts, while others are meant to quickly handle multipage documents using an automatic sheet feeder (instead of a flatbed). In addition to scan speed and the design of the scanner itself, pay attention to its resolution, especially if you'll be scanning highly detailed content, like photos, illustrations, or other graphics. Resolution is measured in dots per inch (dpi). The higher the resolution, the more details you'll see. For example, a document might have 300 x 300 or 2,400 x 2,400 dpi resolution.

Companies like Brother, Epson, and Fujitsu each offer scanners for Windows PCs and Macs that are ideal for a home office. Some of these companies also offer battery-powered, portable scanners that can be used with a laptop computer. To save space (and potentially save money as well), consider purchasing an all-in-one inkjet or laser printer that includes both a flatbed and automatic sheet feeder for its built-in scanner.

Meanwhile, if you're using a smartphone or tablet, one of the fastest and easiest ways to convert a document into a PDF is to use a scanner app to transform its camera into a scanner. When you take a photo of a document, it is saved on your mobile device as a PDF. Some apps also automatically upload it to a popular cloud-based file sharing service.

From the Apple App Store or the Google Play Store, search for "scanner" to find free or low-cost scanner apps, such as:

⇢ *Adobe Scan*: adobe.com/acrobat/mobile/scanner-app.html

⇢ *CamScanner*: camscanner.com/

⇢ *iScanner*: bpmobile.com/apps/scanner

⇢ *Microsoft Lens (Android)*: Google Play link

⇢ *Microsoft Lens (Apple)*: App Store link

⇢ *Scanner Pro*: readdle.com/scannerpro

## Ways You'll Want to Work with PDFs

The following are some of the most common things you'll want to be able to do when working with PDFs. If the application(s) you currently use don't offer this functionality, keep in mind there are countless online tools available (either free or for a fee) via your web browser. Adobe's PDF Online (adobe.com/acrobat/online.html), for instance, offers more than a dozen tools for working with PDF files.

Here's a list of the things you'll want to be able to do with PDFs as a remote worker:

⇢ Annotate a PDF using your own handwriting via a stylus and a touchscreen (or type in comments)

⇢ Compress a PDF to reduce its file size

⇢ Convert/export the file you're working with into a PDF

⇢ Delete pages within a multipage PDF

⇢ Digitally sign a PDF

⇢ Edit PDFs or be able to export them into a commonly used application, like Microsoft Word, Microsoft Excel, Google Docs, or Google Sheets

⇢ Fill in, complete, and distribute PDF forms

⇢ Insert pages into an existing PDF file

⇢ Merge multiple PDFs together into one file

⇢ Print a PDF using your inkjet or laser printer

⇢ Protect a PDF file with a password and/or encryption

⇢ Reorder pages within a PDF file

⇢ Rotate pages within a PDF

⇢ Share a PDF through email, text message, an online collaboration service such as Slack, or an online file sharing service such as Dropbox

⸱▶ Split one PDF into several separate files

⸱▶ Store a PDF locally on your computer or mobile device and sync it with a cloud-based file sharing service you regularly use

## Be Sure to Manage and Organize Your PDF Files

Simply transforming paper documents into PDFs might help you reduce clutter and save space, but unless you organize them properly, you probably won't be able to work with these files efficiently, especially when you have hundreds or thousands of them.

PDFs are much more useful when you're able to quickly locate, view, annotate, edit, print, and share them from any of your computers or mobile devices. Whether you're storing the files locally or on a cloud-based service, use descriptive names for your PDFs so you can recognize them quickly, and create a series of primary folders and subfolders that are properly named and dated. While you can also use the search tool built into the application you use to work with PDFs, storing them in an organized and secure way will make you more efficient.

If you create PDFs of all your receipts so that you can file expense reports and include detailed expense information with your tax returns, or simply because you want to keep track of your monthly spending, you might want to create a master folder called "Receipts," followed by subfolders that divide your receipts into categories, like "Travel," "Food," "Client Entertaining," "Supplies," "Home Office Expenses," "Printing Costs," etc. Next, within each of those subfolders, create an additional subfolder for each year, and another set of subfolders within those, one for each month of the year.

Remember, when your PDFs contain private personal or confidential work information, always take advantage of the password protection and encryption option when creating them. Then even if someone gets their hands on them, the information will not be accessible unless they have the document's password to unlock it.

By creating a detailed and organized folder hierarchy that makes sense for the types of files you'll be storing, you'll get into the habit of maintaining accurate files in a digital format that's ideal for remote workers.

## Digitally Sign Your PDFs

When dealing with digital correspondence and contracts, being able to initial or sign those documents using a stylus and a touchscreen or creating a digital version of your signature and copying it into the document opens up a wide array of ways to use PDFs in your everyday workflow.

In most situations, a digital signature is now considered legally binding. However, you'll want to use a PDF application that makes signed PDFs more secure. In addition to Adobe Acrobat, which you learned about earlier, a company called DocuSign (docusign.com/) offers a collection of easy-to-use software, mobile apps, and online tools that make integrating signatures into PDFs in a secure and trackable way very efficient.

## Consider a PDF's Resolution When Creating It

Yet another consideration when displaying and printing graphics within a PDF is its resolution, measured in dots per inch (dpi). The higher the dpi, the more detailed and clear the content will be when it gets displayed or printed.

Using a lower resolution will result in a smaller file size that makes it faster and easier to share, but detailed graphics and photos won't be as clear, especially when they're printed. Consider what you'll be using the PDF for and how it will be viewed and choose the resolution accordingly when creating or exporting a file into a PDF.

For viewing PDFs on a computer or mobile device screen, 100 dpi is ideal. For printing hard copies from PDFs, go with 300 dpi.

## As a Remote Worker, Always Focus on Security

This chapter touched on using password protection and encryption to keep unauthorized people from being able to access your PDFs. In the next chapter, we'll delve deeper into the need to maintain your privacy and online security. After all, so much of what you'll be doing as a remote worker will involve the internet and cloud-based tools.

While your employer will likely mandate that you use specialized security tools and protocols when working with your company email, file sharing, virtual meeting, payroll and expense reporting, and collaboration tools, you should be taking steps to protect your own privacy, security, computers, and mobile devices when working from home or any other remote location.

## CHAPTER 8

# Effectively Deal with Online Security and Privacy Issues

As a remote worker, much of what you'll be doing involves the use of technology and the internet. And because your personal privacy, the privacy of your employer, and the security of the data you'll be working with are all important, it's your responsibility to ensure that your equipment, the applications you use, the ways you communicate, and the data you work with all remain as secure as possible. This chapter explores many of the ways to make sure your mobile devices, computers, web browsers, applications, and the online tools you rely on all work together to maintain the highest level of security possible.

The first thing you need to understand is that all the tools and applications you'll be using, including your web browser, email client, virtual meeting application, collaboration tools, and cloud-based file sharing services, already have security tools built in to protect you and your information. However, you must first turn on these tools, make sure they're set up properly, and then use them to their utmost advantage.

It's also your responsibility to avoid being careless, which can lead to human error—typically the cause of the biggest data breaches and security issues. You don't need to become a cybersecurity expert to protect yourself and your work. You do, however, need to learn how to use the tools and technology you choose to incorporate into your workflow, and then be diligent about using the security tools built into them.

## The Concerns of an Employer

Before a company begins to rely on remote workers, it's their responsibility to ensure they have the proper infrastructure, bandwidth, and equipment in place to keep their network and data secure. They must also put security tools, protocols, and best practices in place, which each remote employee will need to learn. The employer may or may not dictate which apps remote workers are required to use.

Whether or not remote workers are allowed to choose their own tools, ideally they should keep their personal and work computers and devices separate. This means having a computer, smartphone, and/or tablet that's used exclusively for work and that friends and family members don't have access to.

Also, whether or not it's mandated by an employer, remote workers should take some type of online security awareness training. Free or low-cost training is available through these services and organizations:

- *Beyond Awareness Training ebook from Proofpoint*: proofpoint.com/us/cybersecurity-awareness-hub
- *Cybersecurity Awareness Training by Amazon*: learnsecurity.amazon.com
- *ESET Cybersecurity Training*: eset.com/us/about/

- *SANS Security Awareness Work-from-Home Deployment Kit*: bit.ly/3CowIDi
- *Security First Solutions*: learn.inspiredelearning.com/security-first-sa
- *Security Mentor Security Awareness Training for Remote Workers*: bit.ly/3TkWCPc
- *U.S. Department of Health and Human Services Cybersecurity Awareness Training*: bit.ly/3SYO7K3
- *U.S. Department of Health and Human Services Cybersecurity Essentials Training*: bit.ly/3Ms6nJa

## Start with a Secure Internet Connection

Whether you'll be working from home, from a shared work space, or by using public wifi hotspots from airports, hotels, or cafés, make sure you start with a secure internet connection.

### Add a Firewall to Protect Your Home's Internet

If you'll be working from home, contact your internet service provider (ISP) and make sure you have a firewall and all included security tools activated. According to TechTarget, "A firewall is software or firmware that prevents unauthorized access to a network. It inspects incoming and outgoing traffic using a set of rules to identify and block threats. They are widely considered an essential component of network security."

Beyond activating a firewall, make sure you change the default name and password of your home network, along with the modem and router's admin credentials. You also want to limit access to your wireless network by turning on the password feature, turning on wifi network encryption, and making sure your modem and router's firmware is up-to-date.

Also, when speaking with your ISP, find out if you have the most current modem and router model available and if you're receiving the fastest internet speeds currently being offered. Especially if multiple family members will be relying on your home's wireless network at the same time and you'll have multiple devices connected, it might make sense to upgrade your modem and router.

## Take Advantage of a VPN

Any time you're relying on a wifi internet connection, the computer or mobile device you're using should have an active virtual private network (VPN) application installed and running. This is particularly important when you're using a public wifi hotspot.

Among other things, a VPN will add an extra layer of security to your online activities by hiding your location and encrypting your data. Especially when you're performing any work-related tasks, even something as mundane as managing your email, make sure you have the VPN turned on and active.

Even if you regularly use a smartphone, tablet, laptop, and desktop computer, most VPN services allow you to use the same account on multiple devices for a flat monthly or annual fee. However, you will need to separately install, activate, and configure the VPN application on each of them.

Before subscribing to a VPN service, determine if this is something your employer will provide (or reimburse you for). The cost of a VPN decreases dramatically if you prepay for several years at a time, as opposed to monthly. Also, some VPN services offer additional functionality, such as ad blocking or a password manager. If you often travel internationally, make sure you choose a VPN service that has thousands of servers around the globe—not just in your home country.

While there are many VPN services to choose from, here are a few popular options:

- *CyberGhost VPN*: cyberghostvpn.com/
- *ExpressVPN*: expressvpn.com/
- *NordVPN*: nordvpn.com/
- *Proton VPN*: protonvpn.com/
- *Surfshark*: surfshark.com/

## Use a Password Manager and Strong Passwords

In addition to all the online accounts and services you have in your personal life, as a remote worker, just about every application and service you wind up using for work will require you to create a username and password and link the account to an email address.

Accounts for all job services and applications should be tied to your work email. However, each should have a separate password. You'll want to get into the habit of changing your account passwords on a regular basis (at least once per month, even if this is not something your employer mandates).

As a refresher, all your passwords should be at least eight characters long, include a mix of uppercase and lowercase letters, and include at least one number and one symbol. Use a different password for each account, and don't use passwords that are obvious and common. The most popular and least secure password you can use is the word *password* (or any version of it, such as *Password* or *PassWord*).

Some other passwords you should avoid include:

- abcd1234 (ABCD1234 or 1234ABCD)
- abcdefgh (ABCDEFGH)
- Any animal
- Any color
- Any common name
- Any day of the week or month of the year
- Any superhero
- baseball
- Your child's name
- Your maiden name
- football
- ILoveYou
- Your pet's name
- Princess
- qwerty
- Your spouse's name
- Your birthday or anniversary
- Your company's name
- 11111111
- 11223344
- 12345678
- 22222222
- 33333333
- 87654321

Instead, consider combining two words with random uppercase and lowercase letters and a symbol. For example, instead of the password *superman*, consider *7SupermaN32!*.

The drawback to using different passwords for each of your dozens (potentially hundreds) of separate accounts is that you'll have to remember them. The easiest and most secure way to do this is to use a password manager.

A password manager allows you to create a secure, encrypted, and password-protected database that gets stored in the cloud and will automatically sync and be accessible from all your computers and mobile devices. When a password manager creates a password on your behalf, it can be a long string of random numbers, letters, and symbols. The password manager will remember it for you to log you in to each service when applicable. This means you don't need to rely on traditional words as your passwords, and the passwords you do wind up using will be far more secure.

Be sure to choose a password manager that works with all your devices, so ideally, you want one that has Windows, MacOS, iOS, and Android applications, along with a plug-in or browser extension for the web browser(s) you most commonly use.

Some of the most popular password managers include:

⸱▶ *1Password*: 1password.com/
⸱▶ *Bitwarden*: bitwarden.com/
⸱▶ *Dashlane*: dashlane.com/
⸱▶ *Keeper*: keepersecurity.com/
⸱▶ *LastPass*: lastpass.com/
⸱▶ *NordPass*: nordpass.com/
⸱▶ *Norton 360*: us.norton.com
⸱▶ *RoboForm*: roboform.com/

Several of these companies also offer other online and security software, like a VPN, malware protection, or antivirus software. If you sign up for a service bundle or prepay for a subscription for one, two, or three years at a time, the price drops dramatically. While some of these password managers offer a free plan, this typically only works with one device or limits the number of passwords you can store in your database.

One of the least secure ways to remember your usernames and passwords is to write them down on a piece of paper or a small notebook that you keep next to your computer or carry around with you. Another big no-no is to create a document or spreadsheet called "Passwords" stored on your computer or mobile device. If that list gets lost or stolen, you'll compromise all your accounts simultaneously.

### Install Antivirus and Malware Protection Software

Especially if you use a Windows PC or an Android mobile device, it's essential to have antivirus/malware software—which also detects spyware—always running on your equipment. These days, it's too easy to accidentally download and install a virus or malware. There are several common ways this could happen, such as:

- Responding to a phishing scheme
- Downloading an infected file from someone else
- Granting remote access to your computer (or mobile device) to an unauthorized person
- Having your computer or mobile device hacked into remotely
- Visiting a malicious website that sends harmful files to your computer or is disguised as a website you normally use, so when it asks you to enter your username, password, or credit card details, for example, you're actually providing this information to a hacker

Macs, iPhones, and iPads are also susceptible to viruses and malware, but to a much lesser extent. However, if you'll be using one for work, seriously consider subscribing to and installing Malwarebytes (malwarebytes.com) onto each computer or mobile device. While this application is not owned or operated by Apple, this is the one AppleCare recommends using to detect and fix virus or malware-related issues on an iMac or MacBook.

### How to Tell If Your Computer Has a Virus or Malware

If you suspect your computer or mobile device has acquired a virus or malware, contact your employer's IT department immediately and run a virus/malware removal application. Until you know the situation is under control, don't use it to connect to the internet. Apple users should seriously consider calling AppleCare (800-275-2273) for guidance. Depending on the severity of the situation, you may need a professional cybersecurity expert to make sure your equipment is safe to use without your data or privacy being compromised.

Some of the key indicators that your computer or mobile device may have a virus or malware include:

- Important files are missing, have been renamed, or have moved.
- New applications, files, or folders appear that you never installed.
- Pop-up windows randomly appear.
- Pornographic images replace regular images when you're online.
- The computer does not shut down or restart properly.
- The hard drive seems to be working way too hard and is making unusual sounds (this does not apply to flash drives or SSDs).
- The virus/malware protection application you are running suddenly stops working and will not restart.
- The computer's performance is unusually slow.
- Your computer begins to crash often and for no obvious reason.
- Your computer generates random sounds it's never made before.
- Your computer's built-in webcam turns on at random times when you're not using it.
- Your email client is automatically sending email messages that you didn't write through your account.
- Your social media accounts appear to be compromised, meaning either that you can't access them or posts are being published through your account that you did not create.
- Your web browser's default search engine has been changed or it automatically redirects you to websites you are not trying to visit.

## Use Common Sense to Avoid Phishing Schemes

A phishing scheme tends to arrive as an incoming email that appears to be sent from a reputable company or financial institution you do business with. In reality it's a scam. The subject of the email will include an urgent message, such as "Your account has been compromised," "Your account has been frozen," or "Your credit card information has expired." Another approach is for the subject of the email to announce you've won a lottery, you're receiving a notice to appear in court, you have received an inheritance, or a friend is in dire need of your assistance. The email might also be a receipt for a large purchase or an expensive airline ticket that you never bought.

The subject line is designed to make you open the email immediately by generating an emotional response. When you open it, it may still appear to come from a legitimate company and may include their logo. The body of the message will be designed to persuade you to click on a link, download an attached file, or call a toll-free phone number immediately.

Once you click on the link or download the file, that's when the virus or malware gets into your computer. It might also allow hackers to gain remote access to your computer or automatically begin transferring your private data to them.

If you call the phone number in the email, the scammer will try to persuade you to give them your credit card details, banking information, or enough personal information about yourself so they can steal your identity—such as your full name, address, phone number, date of birth, social security number, driver's license number, passport number, mother's maiden name, or debit card details. If you think you're calling or communicating with a customer service representative for a company you do business with and that person asks for your account username or password, that's a red flag. This is information the company already has within their records, but it's also information a hacker would need to access your account. So if you're asked for this information, there's a good chance you're talking to a cybercriminal who is impersonating an employee from a legitimate company.

Because you will be heavily dependent on email in your role as a remote worker, you must be continuously on the lookout for these phishing schemes. It's not a matter of whether you'll receive one. It's a question of how many you'll get each day. Your strategy should always be to delete all of them without opening. Whatever you do, NEVER respond to them in any way or click on anything in the body of the message or on any attachments.

Phishing emails often claim to come from banks, credit card companies, major airlines, Netflix or other streaming services, courts, Western
Union, Microsoft, Apple, Walmart, Target, Costco, the IRS, your cable TV
service provider, your ISP, your cell phone service provider, or another
well-known company or organization. Again, the goal is to convince you
they're legitimate and get you to respond without thinking about it.

If you get an email that you think *might* be real, do not respond to it.
Instead, call the phone number for that company or organization that you
know is real, because it appears on the back of your credit card, on a printed
bank statement, or on their official website. DO NOT call the phone number listed in the email.

Keep in mind, your intelligence level, education level, or computer
savvy will not protect you from phishing schemes. Every day, many
well-educated and successful people fall victim to these scams. Your best
tool for protecting yourself is to use common sense before opening or
responding to any email that seems at all out of the ordinary. As a remote
worker who relies on email as a primary means of communication, expect
to encounter many different types of these malicious scams in both your
personal and professional email inboxes.

## Use the Security Tools Built into Your Equipment

Let's start by focusing on the security concerns you should have when
working with specific types of equipment and applications.

### Desktop and Laptop Computers

The Windows and Mac operating systems both have built-in security
tools that allow the user to create a username and password required to
unlock the computer when starting up. This is a basic security tool that can
help prevent unauthorized users from gaining access to your computer.
However, you should also take advantage of password protection,
encryption, two-factor authentication, and other security options that are
available in the specific applications you use, as these provide a way to
further protect your data.

While it takes a few extra seconds to sign into your own computer when these security measures are active, it's worth doing, especially on your laptop, which has a greater risk of being lost or stolen when you're working outside your home or a traditional office.

## Mobile Devices

In addition to offering a passcode feature that locks down your smartphone or tablet to keep anyone else from accessing it, most also offer face recognition or fingerprint scanning as an alternate security measure. Again, if you'll be using your mobile device for work, these are basic security measures you will want to activate and use.

It's also a good strategy for iPhone and iPad users to turn on the Find My feature from the iCloud Control menu in Settings, so if your mobile device gets lost or stolen, you can pinpoint its location or remotely erase its contents to prevent it from getting hacked.

## Take Advantage of Security Tools Built into Applications

Simply protecting your computers and mobile devices using basic passwords or passcodes is a good first step, but it's by no means a comprehensive security solution. You should also take advantage of the additional security features built into the applications you'll be using. Let's take a quick look at some of these.

### Password Protection

It's typically possible to turn on a username and password feature for just about any application you'll be using for work. You can also generally add a password to each individual file you'll be working with in each of those applications. So even if everyone in your organization has access to a particular application, you can still limit them from accessing individual files or folders that contain sensitive information.

Yes, adding password protection to individual files and folders means having to enter that password each time you open it. However, it protects the content from hackers as well as from being accessed by someone who receives the file accidentally.

## Use Two-Factor Authentication or an Authenticator App

When it comes to using any cloud-based or other online services, turning on two-factor authentication provides an added level of security. Once this feature is activated, during the log-in process, in addition to entering your username and password, the service will send you an email or text message with a one-time-use code you must also enter to log in.

Thus, even if someone has somehow gotten their hands on your username and password, they'd still need access to your email account or smartphone to retrieve the passcode. Many corporations rely on user authentication through a service like Okta Verify (okta.com/), which offers simplified two-factor authentication for more than 7,000 applications, including many cloud-based applications.

There are also security keys that can be used to prevent unauthorized access to your accounts. Instead of a one-time-use passcode, a physical security key must be inserted into the computer or held near the computer (or mobile device) to gain access.

These security keys can be attached to a key chain or kept in a pocket. They cost $20 to $60 and work with a wide range of websites (and in some cases applications, too) that are commonly used by remote workers. Some can also serve as a password manager. Security keys are available from these companies:

- *Everykey*: everykey.com
- *Google Titan Security Key*: bit.ly/3rTrA5u
- *OnlyKey*: onlykey.io
- *SoloKeys*: bit.ly/3T6tags
- *Thetis*: thetis.io/collections
- *Yubico*: yubico.com/products/

The great thing about these security keys is that if the key itself gets lost or stolen, the person who gains access to it would still need to know your usernames and passwords to log into your accounts. Plus, these keys can be deactivated remotely.

## File Encryption Options

Whether you're using a word processor, spreadsheet, database, or bookkeeping application, in almost every case, individual files can be

## AVOID HUMAN ERROR

Regardless of what applications and online services you'll rely on, even if you use all the latest and most powerful security features, you're still susceptible to problems resulting from human error. A momentary lapse in judgment or a typo could result in a wide range of potential headaches, such as:

- Accidentally downloading and installing a virus or malware

- Sharing a file or folder with the wrong person

- Giving out your username or password for an app or account

- Providing confidential information to a hacker impersonating someone else (via text message, IM, email, or phone)

- Responding to a phishing scheme

No matter how busy you are, before sharing a file or providing confidential information to someone else, confirm it's the correct person. If you're granting permission to someone else on a file sharing service, do not rely on your computer's autocorrect or autofill feature when entering the name or email address. If you start typing John into the To field, your computer may autofill the name or email address of one of the many Johns you know and work with, but it might not be the John you wanted. Before pressing the Send or Confirm button, make sure you've got the right person.

According to phishing training company Phriendly Phishing (phriendlyphishing.com), emailing personal information to the wrong recipient is the cause of 45 percent of all human error data breaches. Unintentionally releasing personal information and failing to use the BCC function on group emails are also common problems.

Another common form of human error is choosing very weak passwords or storing your usernames and passwords insecurely. And one of the biggest, of course, is falling for a phishing scheme. All these potential security risks can be avoided if you use

## AVOID HUMAN ERROR, CONT.

common sense, pay attention to what you're doing, and refuse to respond to unusual requests from other people (especially strangers).

Skill-based human errors and lack of awareness are also common causes of data breaches and security problems. It's essential to learn each of the tools and applications needed for your work and pay attention to the mundane details involved in viewing, sharing, collaborating, and sending files.

password protected *and* encrypted. When a file is encrypted, it scrambles the content and prevents anyone without the proper decryption tool from viewing it, even if they somehow obtain the file.

### Make Sure All Your Applications Are Up-to-Date

The applications you use as a remote worker will often require you to download and install software (or an app) onto your computer and mobile device or access them online via a web browser. You'll find that all the apps you use are continuously being updated by their developers, who are adding new features and functions, including enhancements to their security tools.

For this reason, it's essential to always use the most up-to-date version of all applications. Ideally, you and all your co-workers should be using the same version, especially when collaborating or file sharing, to ensure full compatibility and maximum security.

At least once per month (more often is better), check to see if an update has been issued for the applications you rely on and be sure to download and install those updates. At the same time, confirm that your co-workers and teammates have also installed the latest updates. If new features or functions have been added to the application, discuss how and when your team will use the application's newest capabilities.

### Calendar and Scheduling Applications

When using a group calendar or scheduling application, make sure access to this data is password protected and that someone in your organization is keeping track of assigning and revoking access permissions as employees come and go. Also be mindful of how much personal information you're sharing (such as your location) when adding appointments or other events to a calendar that'll be seen and used by others.

### Cloud-Based File Sharing Services

When using any cloud-based file sharing service, again make sure you're using the most current version of the application (or web browser) needed to access it, and pay careful attention when creating and revoking permissions for individuals to access certain files or folders.

### Online Applications

For any online service, be sure to use a secure password, periodically change your password, and take advantage of two-factor authentication and/or file encryption to ensure the highest level of security.

### Managing Your Email Accounts

If you're managing multiple email accounts from a single email client, make sure you're using the appropriate account to send or respond to messages. You should also follow these 10 strategies to prevent security issues and data breaches:

1. Never open unexpected or unsolicited email attachments.
2. Use a spam filter to weed out unsolicited emails and be sure to customize this feature using the tools provided to you by your email service provider and email client.
3. Be on the lookout for phishing schemes and avoid opening or responding to these messages.
4. Avoid sending highly confidential or sensitive data via email.
5. Do not click on links in emails, especially if they're not from someone you know.
6. Always have antivirus/malware protection software running on the computer or mobile device you use to manage your email.
7. Before hitting Send, always confirm you have entered the recipient's name and email address correctly and double-check you've attached the correct files to the email, if applicable.

8. If you're accessing your email via a public wifi network, always use a VPN.

9. Do not sign up for email lists or promotional emails using your work account.

10. Do not mix your personal and work emails by using the same email account.

## *Browser Plug-Ins*

Every popular web browser has built-in security and privacy tools that you can (and should) activate. In addition, each browser gives you access to a vast library of optional plug-ins and browser extensions that can be installed to provide additional features and functionality. You can add a password manager, VPN, PDF viewer, ad blocker, tracker blocker, integration with other apps (including file sharing services), or a cookie manager.

To discover what optional plug-ins or extensions are available for your favorite web browser, visit these online directories:

- *Chrome:* chrome.google.com/webstore/category/extensions
- *Firefox:* addons.mozilla.org/en-US/firefox
- *Microsoft Edge:* bit.ly/3CUXncr
- *Opera:* addons.opera.com/en
- *Safari:* These are available from the Mac or iOS App Store. For more information on Safari extensions, visit: apple.co/3Vnj5x5.

Based on how you typically use your browser, installing appropriate plug-ins can make your online activities faster and more secure.

## No Security Measures Are 100 Percent Effective

Unfortunately, even if you use every security tool at your disposal and remain extremely diligent when it comes to preventing human error, nothing is 100 percent effective against malicious hackers or data breaches. Through awareness and by taking advantage of the tools available to you, however, you'll be able to prevent many of the problems associated with online security and privacy.

Don't just rely on one tool and assume you're fully protected. Yes, a password manager is useful for maintaining a secure database of your usernames and passwords, but there are other ways a hacker can get this information, especially if you're not careful. And yes, running antivirus and malware protection software is important, but you can still fall victim to a phishing scheme and accidentally install a program that damages your computer.

In addition to the online security risks you'd typically face working from home or a traditional office, other potential dangers exist when you access the internet via a public wifi hotspot. In addition to using a VPN, be sure to use an extra level of common sense and awareness when working with confidential, financial, or proprietary information from remote locations.

As you'll soon find, one of the most common tasks remote workers must handle is participating in video calls and virtual meetings. The focus of the next chapter is to provide you with 25 strategies for hosting and participating in effective virtual meetings as a remote worker.

## CHAPTER 9

# 25 Strategies for Hosting and Participating in Effective Virtual Meetings

According to Webex's "Virtual Meetings in 2022: Everything You Need to Know" (bit.ly/3CtUY7m), "A virtual meeting is a form of communication that enables people in different physical locations to use their mobile or internet-connected devices to meet in the same virtual room. People use virtual meetings in many ways, including . . . collaborating with their distributed workforce."

While a voice-only conference call can be an effective way for groups to communicate, Webex also reported, "The COVID pandemic taught the world many lessons, one of them being that meeting virtually can go a long way towards bridging the gap of physical distance. Many colleagues who had previously only worked together in person were still able to deepen their connection, and in many cases even improve their productivity. Enabling video during virtual meetings can lead to more effective team collaboration, as co-workers can socialize, cooperate, and brainstorm ideas without losing the important elements of body language and facial reactions that can be invaluable when gauging the feelings and opinions of others."

Since the start of the COVID-19 pandemic, the number of annual Zoom meeting minutes is more than 3.3 trillion (as of mid-2022), and more than 300 million people use the platform daily. This represents a 2,900 percent increase compared to prepandemic usage. Other virtual meeting platforms, such as Google Meet and Microsoft Teams, have also experienced a significant rise in usage.

Due to this sudden growth in virtual meeting popularity, 49 percent of remote workers are experiencing "virtual meeting fatigue," according to a 2021 study by Virtira Consulting. Upward of 58 percent of workers (according to passport-photo.online) who participate in virtual meetings continue to be hampered by technical issues. More than half of those who regularly participate in virtual meetings are often disappointed at the lack of planning, focus, and organized facilitation.

As of mid-2022, the five most popular virtual meeting platforms were:

1. *Zoom*: zoom.us
2. *Microsoft Teams*: microsoft.com/en-us/microsoft-teams/
3. *Google Meet*: meet.google.com
4. *Skype*: skype.com/
5. *Slack*: slack.com

In some cases, these services have all but replaced traditional conference rooms. In fact, participating in video calls and virtual meetings often represents a significant part of a remote worker's day, and the average person now spends numerous hours per week in virtual meetings.

Whether you're hosting the meeting, planning the agenda, or simply participating, you can take steps to make your virtual gathering productive and successful. The first group of strategies involves choosing an appropriate hosting service and then selecting, setting up, and using the right equipment. Then the focus shifts to developing the skill set you need to host or participate in effective, efficient virtual meetings.

## 1. Choose the Most Appropriate Virtual Meeting Platform

All the popular virtual meeting platforms allow a group of people to gather in a private area on the internet to exchange information, share ideas, and interact without needing to be in the same physical space. For individual users, setting up an account with one or more of these services is free. However, for the meeting host, depending on the size of the meeting, its duration, and any additional functionality, a paid subscription is typically required.

All the popular platforms, including Zoom, Microsoft Teams, Google Meet, Skype, and Slack, allow anyone to join or host a meeting as long as they have a reliable, high-speed internet connection. Because all are compatible with Windows PCs, MacOS, iOS, and Android, it does not matter what computer or mobile device each person in the group is using. While each service has its own app that makes hosting or participating in a virtual meeting simple, you can also go through its website.

Establishing an account takes just a few minutes, but you must make certain that everyone who wants to attend the meeting has registered with that service. And since each offers slightly different functionality and security/privacy tools—although they all achieve the same result in the end—it's important to choose the service that meets the needs of your team or organization.

You can hold virtual meetings with a handful, dozens, or even hundreds of participants. And while a video meeting is taking place, a private text-based chat room is also available, so people who are not currently speaking can interact.

As a remote worker, especially if you are an independent contractor or freelancer, you'll often need to participate in virtual meetings hosted by different services, so you will need to register for and learn how to use several popular virtual meeting platforms. Because the user interface for each service is slightly different, don't wait until five minutes before the meeting before you sign in and begin trying to figure out how to access the meeting room with your webcam, microphone, and speakers (or headphones/earbuds) properly configured. While a mobile device is easier to set up and use for a video call or virtual meeting, it's a good idea to ensure you have a good internet connection and the correct meeting details before the last minute, so sign into the meeting a few minutes early.

## 2. Use the Most Current Version of the Application or Web Browser

Regardless of which virtual meeting platform you wind up using, like any other app, they all regularly release updates, so make sure you have the latest version running on your equipment, or the latest version of your web browser installed if you're going through their website.

## 3. Prepare Your Computer or Mobile Device

All the popular virtual meeting platforms require each meeting participant to have access to a fast and reliable internet connection, preferably wifi or 5G, as opposed to a basic 3G or 4G LTE cellular connection. However, if a high-speed internet connection is not available, most services allow participants to use any telephone (including landline phones) to call into a meeting, but the call will be audio only.

Especially if you use multiple virtual meeting platforms, sign into the platform at least five minutes before each meeting. These days, you'll come off as unprepared, not at all tech-savvy, and rude if you show up to a meeting late, or if you sign into a meeting but can't be heard or seen due to a technical glitch, which is why you should test everything a few minutes before the meeting starts. Confirm that your account settings are correct and your equipment is configured for that platform. Check that the camera, microphone, and speakers are all working properly (if you're on your computer). Occasionally, you may need to reboot your computer to get it to work properly.

## 4. Include Your Account Information and Profile Photo

Each of the virtual meeting platforms requires each meeting participant to create a profile. This will include your name and a profile photo. Especially if you'll be meeting with a larger group of people, or people you're not well-acquainted with, it's considered polite to display your full name and photo in your profile. That way, if another participant clicks on your profile, they can quickly see your job title, company name, phone number, and email address.

When choosing your profile photo, use one that resembles a professional headshot. You should be wearing professional business attire. In other words, don't use a vacation photo or full-body photo, or an old photo that looks nothing like what you look like today.

All other meeting participants will be able to see your name and profile photo, along with all the information in your profile, so only share details that you want your employer, co-workers, teammates, or other meeting participants to know about you.

### USING A FREE VS. PAID VIRTUAL MEETING PLATFORM ACCOUNT

Each virtual meeting platform tries to differentiate itself based on the additional functionality it offers to its paid subscribers. While anyone can set up an account with almost any platform and participate in meetings for free, they might not have access to features like the ability to record a meeting, real-time closed captioning, virtual backgrounds, or special effect filters.

Meanwhile, when it comes to hosting meetings, a free account often limits how many meetings you can host per month, how long each meeting can be, and how many attendees can participate simultaneously. Other hosting features may also be locked.

Depending on how you'll be using one or more virtual meeting platforms, determine what functionality you need and whether you'll require a paid subscription.

## 5. Choose the Best Camera, Microphone, and/or Headset

The whole purpose of virtual meetings is to allow all participants to be seen and heard. While all computers and mobile devices now have built-in cameras, speakers, and microphones, the quality of these components may not be adequate.

You may find it useful to connect an external, high-resolution camera to your computer or mobile device, along with an external microphone and/or speakers. For added privacy and better audio clarity, many people use wired or wireless headphones, earbuds, or headsets during their meetings. Some of these also have a built-in microphone, and many offer noise-cancelation technology that removes ambient noise (and wind noise if you're outside).

Logitech (logitech.com/en-us/products/webcams.html) and Creative (us.creative.com/wfh/#look-professional), for example, offer a wide range of high-resolution webcams that connect to a computer via its USB or USB-C port.

Some of the best noise-canceling headphones and earbuds (with built-in microphones) come from the following companies:

- *Apple*: apple.com/airpods/
- *Bang & Olufsen*: bang-olufsen.com/en/us/headphones
- *Bose Headphones and Earbuds*: bose.life/3VsHoti
- *Creative*: us.creative.com/wfh
- *Master & Dynamic*: masterdynamic.com/collections/all
- *Samsung*: samsung.com/us/mobile-audio/galaxy-buds2/
- *Sennheiser*: sennheiser-hearing.com/en-US/headphones
- *Sony Earbuds and Headphones*: bit.ly/3VrxiZW

Plan on spending between $50 and $200 for a high-resolution, external webcam. Wireless headphones or earbuds with noise-canceling technology that offer excellent sound quality and a style that's suitable for work will cost between $100 and $400.

Especially if you'll be using a smartphone or tablet in public or noisy locations, you'll want to invest in a good pair of wireless headphones or earbuds.

## 6. Focus on Lighting

When you're participating in a video call or virtual meeting, the camera should ideally be positioned in front of your face at about eye level. To avoid unflattering shadows, your primary light source should be directly in front of you, or place separate light sources on either side of your face.

Avoid having the primary light source directly over your head. That will create shadows below your eyes, nose, ears, and chin, which can be very unflattering.

Also refrain from positioning yourself in front of a window (during the day). When your primary light source is behind you, shining directly into the camera, you'll wind up looking like a dark silhouette.

There are all sorts of lights you can get to brighten up your face and upper body when you're participating in virtual meetings. A ring light, which goes around your webcam, is designed to shine an even light on your entire face without creating any shadows. There are also lights that clip onto your computer monitor or laptop or attach to your desk, which you can reposition as needed.

The Lume Cube Edge Light (bit.ly/3VqNBWY) is a circular light on an adjustable arm that clamps onto a desk or table, which you can then position however you want. The company also offers a selection of tiny RGB light panels that can attach to a computer, as well as cordless ring lights. These products allow you to shine more light onto your face and your surroundings when you participate in a video call or virtual meeting.

To discover many more lighting options, type in "virtual meeting light" on your favorite search engine. Ideally, you want a light that you can manually adjust the light's temperature and intensity (brightness), plus easily position it at the best angle to brighten up your face and upper body while avoiding unwanted shadows.

Keep in mind that anytime you're using an artificial light source, anything shiny you're wearing (such as eyeglass frames or jewelry) could cause distracting reflections for the people looking at you on their screens. Use the video preview window offered by each virtual meeting or video calling platform to make sure you look your best.

If you wear prescription glasses, consider ordering a pair with lenses that have an antireflective coating. While you're at it, also consider adding a blue light filter to the lenses. This will help prevent eyestrain when look-ing at a computer screen for extended periods of time.

## 7. Select an Appropriate Background

When people spend a lot of time in video calls and virtual meetings, their minds start to wander. Instead of paying attention to the people they're speaking with, they wind up focusing on whatever's behind the other participants. Always check your background to make sure whatever people can see is visually appealing, appropriate, and not too distracting.

Some people opt to set up a solid color background behind them, because keeping the background as simple as possible is a professional approach. However, if you opt to showcase part of your home office, make sure the background is not too busy. Yes, people will try to figure out what books are on your bookshelf, what types of plants are growing behind you, and what's written on your whiteboard. Many webcams use a wide-angle lens, so make sure that anything you don't want people to see is not within the camera's range—either behind you or to either side.

If you do use a solid color background, make sure to wear clothing in a contrasting color, so you don't blend in—or clash. Either would create a visual distraction and divert attention from your contributions to the meeting.

## 8. Take Advantage of Filters, Virtual Backgrounds, and Other Special Features

Many of the virtual meeting and video calling platforms offer filters, virtual backgrounds, and other effects that can alter your appearance, make it seem like you're in a different location, or create whimsical animated avatars to represent you.

Of course, some of these features are not suitable for work, but the ability to enhance your complexion, adjust your eyes so it appears you're looking directly into the camera, or create a more visually appealing back-ground are features remote workers often use.

Feel free to experiment with the various effects offered by the vir-tual meeting platform, but make sure you try them out before you use them in an important meeting. Also make sure they are appropriate for a work situation, not potentially offensive, and not distracting to other participants.

Any time you'll be participating in a virtual meeting with people you don't regularly work with, consider using a blurred background so it'll be harder for other attendees to figure out where you are or what type of remote location you work from.

## 9. Configure and Test the Virtual Meeting Application

Regardless of how many virtual meetings and video calls you participate in per day, get into the habit of logging into the virtual meeting platform at least five minutes early. Test out the camera and microphone you'll be using (even if they're built in) and make sure you have the correct URL and log-in information for the meeting.

Once you know your equipment is working, use the video preview window to check your appearance, the lighting, and the background. What you see in this preview window is exactly what other meeting participants will see, so if your hair is messy, your shirt looks wrinkled, or your face can't be seen clearly due to poor lighting or unwanted shadows, fix it quickly.

After each meeting, always make sure you disconnect from the meeting *and* log out of the platform. Confirm that your camera and microphone are deactivated before you say or do anything that could cause problems if the other people in the meeting overheard you.

## 10. Develop or Adhere to Virtual Meeting Protocols and Etiquette

Every company and team have their own formal and informal protocols or etiquette guidelines for what's considered appropriate during a virtual meeting. Some companies or team leaders insist that everyone keeps their cameras turned on throughout every meeting, even when they're only listening to a presenter.

It's also common for organizations to have guidelines about how people should interact when someone else is presenting. If you have a question or opinion, are you supposed to just unmute your microphone and blurt out what's on your mind, or should you click on the icon to raise your virtual hand and wait to be called on? Or perhaps you should type your question or idea in the live chat accompanying the virtual meeting?

Some team leaders allocate time at the start of each meeting for small talk before delving into the core agenda. You'll want to figure out what's considered proper etiquette for your company or team and adhere to those guidelines.

Because you're interacting in a virtual environment as opposed to in person, actions and words can easily be interpreted differently. If you're in a virtual meeting while someone else is presenting, and you get an incoming call or text on your phone, it is blatantly obvious when you look away from the camera and focus on something else. It's easier for someone to accidentally convey body language or actions that demonstrate disinterest via a video call or virtual meeting than it is during an in-person meeting where everyone can see everything that's happening.

Likewise, if someone else is presenting and you suddenly turn off your camera (even though you're still listening), it could be perceived as disrespectful or rude. It's also easy to forget that even when you're not actively speaking during a virtual meeting, all the participants can still see you when your camera is turned on.

As for audio, during most group meetings, it's considered appropriate to mute your microphone whenever you're not speaking. When your microphone is muted, a special icon will appear on the screen. Remember to unmute it before you begin talking, and make sure there are no distracting sounds in the background.

Finally, before each meeting, make sure you're properly prepared and enter the meeting on time or several minutes early. It can be very disruptive if people join after the virtual meeting has started. Also, if you know you'll be presenting during the meeting, have your notes, PowerPoints, or other content queued up and ready.

If you're a team leader or meeting host, you must make the meeting objectives clear, set the agenda, discuss the protocols for participants, and pay attention to the time so the meeting does not run too long.

## 11. Encourage Use of the Chat Feature

To streamline how people interact during a virtual meeting, it often makes sense to encourage them to share their questions, comments, and ideas in the live chat associated with the meeting. This is typically far less disruptive unless the host opens the forum for a discussion or Q&A session.

Keep in mind that the chat can be seen by all participants unless you send a private message to one or more people. If you do use the private message feature, make sure you select the right recipients and double-check the settings so you don't inadvertently send the message to the entire group.

Maintain the same level of professionalism in the chat as you do in the virtual meeting. Refrain from making comments, jokes, or criticisms that could offend people or be misinterpreted. Depending on your company's culture, it may also be considered inappropriate to use emojis or share photos or memes in this forum during a meeting.

When used correctly, the chat feature can be used to solicit questions, gauge participants' opinions, or encourage relevant interactions in a way that saves time and does not interrupt the flow of the meeting.

## 12. Schedule Appropriately and Invite the Right People

Research conducted by passport-photo.online indicates that the best day to schedule a virtual meeting is on a Tuesday, while the worst days are typically Mondays and Fridays. As for timing, most people prefer them in the morning or right before lunch. Also, if you expect everyone to actively participate, it's best to keep the number of people at the meeting to 10 or fewer.

Beyond these guidelines, prior to each meeting, it's the leader's responsibility to:

- Determine who should attend
- Decide how long the meeting will last
- Send out the invitations (as far in advance as possible)
- Set and share the meeting's agenda (also in advance)
- Clearly indicate what's expected of the participants

While you must take care to invite all the essential people to your meeting, it's equally important to invite *only* those people. If people's days are frequently disrupted by being invited to mandatory meetings that are completely irrelevant to their work, morale and productivity in your organization will crater.

## 13. Set an Ideal Meeting Length and Create an Agenda

If a virtual meeting is boring, disorganized, or goes off-topic, participants are more apt to get distracted, begin multitasking, and pay less attention to the topic being discussed. When virtual meeting attendees lose focus, they often begin checking their email, messaging other people, looking at their social media feeds, or reading the news—all of which affect the meeting's effectiveness.

It's best to keep meetings as short as possible—15, 30, or 60 minutes. Without multiple breaks, meetings that go longer than an hour tend to be far less productive and interfere too much with participants' already busy schedules.

The meeting's host should create a detailed agenda in writing that explains the meeting's purpose, goals, and format, and what's expected of the participants. All invitees should receive a copy of the agenda in advance.

Figure 9.1 on page 159 is an example of a virtual meeting agenda. This agenda can typically be included with the meeting invitation, which is created and sent via either a group scheduling application or the virtual meeting platform that'll be used to host the meeting. It can also be sent to invitees later via text message or email.

## 14. Take Proper Security Precautions

Depending on the meeting's agenda and attendees, it may be necessary to use additional security tools offered by the hosting service beyond simply requiring remote workers to use a virtual private network (VPN) when going online.

To help prevent unauthorized people from attending virtual meetings, each participant must treat their account information for the platform as securely as they would their online banking information. This means keeping their username and password secure. It's also important that participants not share the meeting links in any public forums, whether they're within their organization or on social media.

FIGURE 9.1—**Virtual Meeting Invitation and Agenda**

| | |
|---|---|
| Meeting Topic | |
| Goal/Objective | |
| Leader/Host | |
| Date | |
| Time | |
| Duration | |
| List of Invitees | |
| Meeting Website URL & Password (if applicable) | |

### Example of a 30-Minute Virtual Meeting Agenda

| | |
|---|---|
| 0:00-0:03 | Introductions and review of agenda |
| 0:03-0:13 | Presentation by [insert name] |
| 0:13-0:18 | Q&A session with presenter |
| 0:18-0:23 | Presentation by [insert name] |
| 0:23-0:25 | Q&A session with presenter |
| 0:25-0:30 | Wrap-up, recap, and discussion of next steps or call to action for participants |

If possible, the meeting host should set up a virtual waiting room that all attendees must enter before they can access the meeting itself. For regularly scheduled meetings (daily, weekly, or monthly), while it may be easier to use the same meeting ID or link, it should still be changed periodically, especially if there have been personnel changes within your company.

In addition to attendees being sent a meeting invite, it's often possible to create a unique password that they must provide to access the meeting. To prevent unwanted guests, the meeting host should take attendance at the start of the meeting and then lock it down so no one else can enter once it's formally underway.

Another useful security precaution is to turn on the meeting platform's alert feature, so the host is notified whenever someone enters or exits the meeting. Meanwhile, if the meeting is being recorded, the host should remind participants of this, even though an icon indicating the recording will appear on everyone's screen.

As a participant, whenever you receive a virtual meeting invite, check that it's from someone you know and trust, and that you're not required to download or install anything during the RSVP process. Sending out fake meeting invites that include a virus or malware is one way hackers trick people into giving them access to their computers or mobile devices. If your organization typically uses Zoom, but you suddenly receive a meeting invite for Google Meet or Skype from a co-worker, consider whether it could be a security threat.

While all the virtual meeting platforms use cutting-edge security tools, all participants should be using the latest version of the application. If you're going through the website, use the most recent version of the web browser that's recommended by the hosting platform. Some security features and other meeting tools will not work with some less popular or older versions of certain web browsers.

If security is an ongoing issue for your team or organization, consider requiring all virtual meeting participants to engage in some form of online security awareness training. Numerous organizations offer free or low-cost training and information in this area, including:

- *Google Meet Security & Privacy for Users*: bit.ly/3ex2mH1
- *KnowBe4*: info.knowbe4.com
- *LinkedIn Learning*: bit.ly/3CU2oBX
- *SANS Virtual Conferencing Safely and Securely*: bit.ly/3Msj7Q0
- *Security and Microsoft Teams*: bit.ly/3Tiucp5
- *Security at Zoom*: explore.zoom.us/en/trust/security/
- *Slack Security*: slack.com/solutions/security
- *U.S. Department of Homeland Security CISA Guidance for Securing Video Conferencing*: bit.ly/3CVjhwh
- *Zoom Security Basics*: youtube.com/watch?v=dgs9mjnycaE

## 15. Dress for a Business Meeting, Not a Pajama Party

Especially if you're working from home, it's easy to dress casually or even just roll out of bed and start your workday before showering and getting dressed. However, remote workers are expected to be available during business hours for impromptu video calls and virtual meetings. So you should get into the habit of putting on casual business attire (or whatever your employer expects) every morning so you don't get caught wearing pajamas or sweatpants during work hours.

## 16. Determine When to Speak and When to Listen

It's common sense that when you're a presenter in a virtual meeting, you're expected to speak—with well-thought-out and prepared information to share. Everyone else is expected to listen, and sometimes take notes.

But there's a difference between active and passive listening. Active listening is when you're watching the presenter, paying close attention to what they're saying, and trying to learn as much as possible. Passive listening means you can hear what the presenter is saying, but your mind is focused on something else or you're trying to multitask during the meeting. In general, as a virtual meeting participant, you're expected to be an active listener (and keep your microphone muted).

However, there will be times when you're encouraged to voice an opinion, share information, ask a question, or engage with other attendees. How you do this should be dictated by the meeting host or presenter. When you're the presenter, remember that when open discussion is taking place, questions are being asked, or other people are giving their opinions, it's your turn to be an active listener.

Anytime you choose to speak up, stay on topic, convey your ideas in the clearest and most succinct way possible, and refrain from harshly criticizing someone else's opinions or ideas. Meetings should be a safe space, without fear of being ridiculed or dismissed.

## 17. Look into the Camera and Don't Get Distracted

Camera placement is important when participating in a virtual meeting. While some cameras and video meeting services will automatically keep you centered on the screen, even if you move around, position the camera so that when you're facing forward and watching the meeting on your screen, you're also looking into the camera, so you seem actively engaged and attentive.

If your camera is positioned too high or low, it'll appear as if you're looking off into space and not paying attention. During long meetings, it's common for our minds to wander, which causes us to look off in various directions or have our attention drawn away by something happening off-screen.

While you want to stay focused on the meeting, make sure your eyes are looking into the camera, so it appears to everyone else that you're fully present and attentive.

## 18. Distribute the Agenda and a List of Participant Expectations

If you're hosting a virtual meeting, in addition to providing a detailed agenda along with the invitation, make it clear if you want invitees to prepare something in advance. If the meeting is being held to discuss customer service policies and procedures, you might ask attendees to prepare and submit via email a list of three ideas or strategies for improving the company's customer service practices prior to the meeting, stating that these ideas will be read and discussed during the meeting.

By asking people to prepare in advance, you'll save a lot of time during the meeting and eliminate the early steps involved in exercises like brainstorming sessions.

At the conclusion of a meeting, briefly recap what you covered and then provide a call to action (with a deadline) for all participants, so it's clear what they're expected to do next and when they need to complete those tasks. You could say "For next week's meeting, everyone please prepare a detailed progress report on the project you're currently working on and be able to present to the group a two-minute summary of your progress and achievements for this quarter."

## 19. Allocate Time for Pleasantries

While allocated meeting times should focus on the agenda, consider opening the virtual meeting room 15 minutes before the formal start of a meeting, or keep it open for 15 minutes after a meeting concludes, so invitees can interact informally. Make this time optional, so people can choose to participate if it fits in their schedule.

Aside from asking how everyone is doing in your opening statement, you'll save a lot of time by confining personal chat to these informal sessions, unless it's relevant to the meeting's purpose and fits into the agenda.

A better use of everyone's time is to schedule virtual lunch breaks or happy hours where teams or co-workers can meet and interact socially online without discussing work.

## 20. The Meeting Host Needs to Maintain Control

Especially when a group of 5, 10, or more people are meeting online, it's very easy for a discussion to veer off-topic and for people to quickly lose focus. While everyone should be mindful of what they're contributing to a meeting and how relevant what they're sharing is, it's ultimately the host's responsibility to keep the meeting on track.

When the host explains the agenda, they should set expectations about what level of interaction is expected or required from attendees, such as:

- "Please keep your microphones muted during the presentation and hold your questions until the end."
- "Please use the virtual hand raise command during the presentation if you have a question or comment and wait for the presenter to call on you."
- "During today's meeting, please post all your questions and opinions in the text-based chat, and we'll address them at the appropriate time."

As a meeting participant, follow the guidelines you're given, no matter how pressing your question, thought, or idea seems to you. Failing to do so and continually interrupting the host could disrupt the flow of the meeting and waste everyone's time.

## 21. Don't Become an Interruptor or Distractor

Again, to maintain the steady flow of a meeting and stay within your preset time limit, it's important to avoid interruptions and distractions—whether they're deliberate or accidental. Someone leaving their microphone unmuted while their dog is barking in the background could become a huge distraction for everyone.

Other common distractions happen when:

→ People log in late to a meeting.

→ One or more people log in without first testing their equipment, only to discover their camera or microphone isn't working. Then they must sign off, reboot, and log in again, while everyone else waits for them. By the time everyone is ready to go, five or more minutes have already been wasted of the 15-minute meeting.

→ Participants ask questions that have already been answered or that are irrelevant to the focus of the meeting.

→ The presenter is not properly prepared with their information and their slide deck or does not know how to properly share their screen with participants.

→ One or more people have a slow or unstable internet connection, which keeps them from being seen and heard clearly.

## 22. Assign Someone to Take Notes

When a virtual meeting goes well, a lot of information can be presented and shared in a relatively short time. To ensure everyone stays on the same page and remembers all the pertinent information, it's often useful to assign someone to take notes and then share them with the other attendees afterward. This is also useful for invitees who miss a meeting due to illness or a scheduling conflict and who don't have time to watch the whole recorded meeting.

One option is to turn on the closed captioning feature that most virtual meeting platforms offer, create a transcript of the meeting, and then have someone edit down that transcript into a condensed meeting summary.

Many third-party applications that work in conjunction with Zoom, Google Meet, Microsoft Teams, and other platforms use an AI assistant to automatically record meeting notes, gather transcriptions, and then create a summary of the meeting. Some of these subscription or fee-based applications include:

→ *Fathom AI Notetaker*: fathom.video

→ *Fellow*: fellow.app/lp/zoom-note-taking-app

⸱▸ *Fireflies*: fireflies.ai/integrations/videoconferencing/zoom
⸱▸ *Otter Voice Meeting Notes*: get.otter.ai
⸱▸ *Sembly*: sembly.ai

## 23. Pay Attention to the Clock and Be Mindful of People's Time

Whether you're the host or an active participant, pay attention to the clock during each meeting and don't fall into that "just one more thing" mentality that often causes meetings to run over. People have busy schedules and often have to run from one meeting to the next. When your meeting runs late, it either forces people to leave early (and potentially miss important information) or it disrupts the rest of their schedule.

When your scheduled meeting time comes to an end, assume that the participants have something else scheduled immediately following it. Don't try to extend the meeting if you still have more to discuss. Instead, find a convenient time in everyone's schedule for a follow-up.

## 24. Record the Meeting for People Who Missed It

Using a human notetaker or AI assistant designed to create meeting summaries, it's easy to keep text records of meetings. However, many organizations opt to record the virtual meetings and make them available to participants and executives who were unable to attend. Recording a meeting provides a resource people can refer to in the future, although it's common courtesy (and in some states a legal requirement) to inform all participants when a meeting is being recorded.

## 25. Follow Up with a Summary and Call to Action

At the end of a meeting, most people will be anxious to sign off and go about their workday, so it's useful for the host to follow up after a meeting with a summary of what was covered and a call to action that describes what each participant needs to do. Each task should be spelled out and have a deadline associated with it, so everyone knows what's expected of them moving forward.

## CHAPTER 10

# The Psychological Aspect of Working Remotely

While most people truly enjoy the many benefits of being a remote worker, one of the most common drawbacks is experiencing feelings of isolation and loneliness, especially if you're accustomed to a busy office environment.

Everyone has their own methods for combating these emotions, but you'll want to deal with them immediately, before they develop into deeper feelings of depression or anxiety. One of the best ways to reduce stress as a remote worker is to maintain a well-organized work space and to establish a regular daily routine.

"When working from home, it's essential to have a routine, so you don't lose track of time. Make a daily routine that includes time for intensive work, breaks, and goal setting. Your employment may need the creation of separate time slots for distinct duties. For example, you can only respond to emails from 8 A.M. to 9 A.M.; then work on your project from 10 A.M. to noon. Your remote working days will be less likely to be interrupted if you have more structure," said psychiatrist Dr. David McConaghy.

Cynthia Halow (personalitymax.com/) is a licensed psychologist who specializes in industrial and organizational psychology. She said, "For many, remote work has been the norm since the beginning of the COVID-19 pandemic. Many people have adapted to this new setup. But there are some who are still experiencing some challenges with it. For one, you must be able to draw the line between your personal and professional life. In most work-from-home arrangements, there will be many instances of overlap between these two. Work-life balance should be a big concern. Stick to your assigned shift schedule and then turn off your work devices as soon as you log out from work. At times, you may need to fight off the tendency to go back for items that you want done."

She added, "The lack of personal connection is also one concern. Virtual social interactions are a common thing now. Most companies do this to compensate for in-person social gatherings and to help people develop bonds and build relationships. Meetings and conferences are now held via various digital applications. Even team dinners and get-togethers are now held virtually. The world is changing, so we must prepare for and accept these changes. They will be the future, and we need to embrace the new work culture."

Psychologist Claire Grayson is a cofounder of PersonalityMax along with Halow. She explained, "Since the rise of remote work, more and more people are leaving their physical offices to work from the comfort of their homes and other remote locations. While many people say very positive things about the freedom that comes with remote working, I do believe that in some ways, remote work can do more harm than good.

"Humans are social by nature. I think this is something that many have pushed to the background as they try to keep up in the fast-paced world. And for people who live alone, working remotely further relegates them away from seeing and socializing with people. I often tell my clients that loneliness is a fickle little thing that creeps up before you're fully aware of it. It immerses you completely, and you get used to the idea of being alone so much that your mindset and lifestyle change. Of course, loneliness also has a direct link to depression and anxiety, and we know how hard it is to crawl out of the dark hole that is depression."

To combat loneliness, Grayson recommends maintaining physical relationships, going for regularly scheduled walks, joining a society composed of like-minded people, creating a work routine and sticking to it, and not getting lost in your work. "If you feel like you need someone to talk to, don't hesitate to reach out to an expert," she added. "Even speaking with a therapist is good socialization."

## Expert Advice from Miriam Groom, an Industrial and Organizational Therapist and HR Strategist

Miriam Groom specializes in coaching and counseling, employee experience, recruitment, retention, and employee development. She works as a leader in talent management for KPMG and founded a national career counseling practice, called Mindful Career (mindfulcareer.ca). In this interview, she shares her advice about how to overcome the pitfalls and challenges of being a remote worker.

*What are the most common psychological or emotional pitfalls related to transitioning from a traditional office job to becoming a remote worker?*

*Groom*: "Every individual will experience this transition a bit differently. It really has to do with their personality type. The way people manage their time autonomously and the boundaries they set for themselves are two of the major issues that can cause a lot of stress.

"For instance, someone with a perceiving personality type—a type that prefers relaxed, spontaneous schedules, as described by Myers-Briggs—may have difficulty with the lack of formal boundaries keeping them in check. These people might end up feeling overwhelmed by too much unstructured free time. Someone who relates more to the judging personality type, characterized by a task-oriented and 'type A' personality, however, may find themselves working overtime and on weekends because they can't separate work from life. Both types can, however, adapt to remote work given the right tools and by learning new behaviors."

*How can someone deal with the stresses of having to separate their personal and professional life once they begin working from home?*

*Groom*: "Those who end up working overtime and on weekends can consider scheduling breaks for activities like eating lunch, doing 15-minute meditation sessions, or simply closing their computer for a few minutes. It sounds obvious, but making personal time a formalized 'to-do' item can definitely help people feel more balanced. It's one thing to tell yourself that it's time to stop working, but it's another thing to work it into your schedule as a real activity."

*Without supervision from superiors or co-workers, what strategies can you share for staying focused and motivated as a remote worker?*

*Groom*: "Again, the strategy will depend on the individual and their personality. Someone with perceiving traits will have a harder time staying motivated, as they tend to procrastinate and want to do things that are fun rather than follow rules and check things off their list. For these individuals, asking for routine check-ins with their team can help them stay on track.

"Ultimately, it comes down to understanding your workstyle and personality so you can identify approaches that make sense for you. There are many tools to discover your working style, such as psychometric tests and other assessments."

*When someone starts working remotely, they often feel isolated from their co-workers and no longer part of their organization's culture. What should be done to counteract this?*

*Groom*: "A sense of belonging is important for all employees, be they extroverted or introverted. Replicating an in-person environment isn't always possible, but people still need to try to bond. This can include a 15-minute 'virtual coffee break' each day or making plans to meet in person if the situation allows it. Companies should encourage casual chatting and virtual hangouts, if they don't infringe on workflow or take up too much time."

*What are some of the signs that someone is not adjusting well to being a remote worker from an emotional or psychological standpoint? What should they do about this?*

*Groom*: "It can be hard to identify signs when you can't see a person's face. Nonverbal cues can communicate a lot, however, so I recommend having meetings with the camera on so you can gauge people's facial expressions and body language.

"Some signs of isolation can include answering fewer emails as well as seeming less engaged and less involved in meetings and other virtual activities. People expressing sadness and depression are, obviously, some of the most obvious signs they need help adapting to remote work."

*If someone is having trouble focusing on their work as a remote worker, what are some strategies for regaining and maintaining their focus?*

*Groom*: "There are different solutions to this problem depending on the psychological profile of the person in question. Someone with a judger personality type may feel overwhelmed without the structure they were once used to. Helping them create a roadmap and then triaging activities so they know where to prioritize their time can help them focus and stay on track. A person with a perceiver personality may end up lacking the discipline needed to perform uninteresting tasks, so helping them identify low-hanging fruit and take baby steps when tackling large projects can help them feel more focused and productive."

*When someone takes breaks from work during their workday as a remote worker, what are some of the things they should do to stay healthy from an emotional/psychological standpoint?*

*Groom*: "Meditation, breathing exercises, and physical exercise are all really important. While many of us have sedentary lifestyles in general, going to a physical workplace usually requires more movement compared to waking up and flipping open a laptop. People working from home should be prompted to get up and move around throughout the day. Scheduled exercise can be a companywide policy if these breaks are kept short so that people don't skip them."

*How can someone overcome anxiety related to being a remote worker and having to take on and learn new skills to meet their work obligations?*

*Groom*: "When it comes to anxiety, it's critical to identify your stress triggers and then work from there. Different people become anxious for different reasons, so there's no one-size-fits-all solution here. Working with a career counselor can help someone figure out why they feel so anxious and how to deal with it.

"Some remote work-related anxiety may come from having to learn different project management software, time tracking tools, and so on. A creative with a perceiving personality type, for example, might find tracking their hours and creating productivity reports for their remote manager incredibly anxiety-producing. They can consider talking to their supervisor to see if there's a work-around for this, or they can ask a colleague to take these tasks off their hands if applicable.

"Finally, honesty is the best policy, and explicitly telling a manager 'These new administrative tasks are making me anxious' can be the best way to manage the issue."

*Are there specific scheduling techniques you'd recommend when it comes to balancing work and professional life as a remote worker?*

*Groom*: "Yes! Schedule downtime in your calendar in the same way you would schedule a meeting. These breaks can include your lunch hour, a quick break to run an errand, or even just 15 minutes to stretch and re-center yourself.

"Because people can sometimes get caught up in virtual meetings all day, it's also important to book meeting-free time to allow for your individual work. Finally, consider scheduling 15-minute meetings as a default, as 30- to 60-minute meetings are often unnecessary."

*How can someone overcome the overwhelming urge to constantly check their work emails, voice mails, and text messages during their off-hours?*

*Groom*: "People get addicted to checking work emails the same way they get addicted to social media and other online distractions. Understand that screens are addictive, and consider turning off notifications on evenings and weekends. It's important to take our lives and our health as seriously as we take our work."

*From a psychological standpoint, what are some of the biggest mistakes you see first-time remote workers make?*

Groom: "The list is long. Working into the night, not leaving the house, not having any kind of routine (including hygiene routines), not taking breaks, and failing to implement time management techniques are among the most common. Working in a physical environment typically forces us to follow strict routines that include commuting each day, taking lunch breaks, and following a lot of external cues and prompts. We can re-create these on our own in a remote environment, but it takes self-awareness, deliberate effort, and some relearning."

*If someone must share their home office work space with a spouse, partner, roommate, or even their kids, what tips can you offer for maintaining their sanity, privacy, and avoiding too much close contact during their workday and off-hours?*

Groom: "Like in most situations, communication is key. It's important to kindly tell the people you live with that you need a certain amount of space and quiet time to work. When it comes to small kids, I recommend using color-coded signs (think red light, green light) rather than a written sign so they can see when you are available. I sound repetitive, but scheduling time to go for brief walks can really help you to re-center, and it relieves some of the stress that can come from sharing a work space. Finally, noise-canceling headphones are always a great investment."

*In your opinion, what is the ideal personality type for a successful remote worker? If someone does not inherently have this type of personality, can they develop it?*

Groom: "Anyone can be a successful remote worker if they understand themselves and employ strategies to improve their output and avoid feelings of overwhelm or isolation. We often assume that the introverted judger personality type thrives in a remote environment, but they are prone to overworking and lacking that boundary between work time and personal time.

"Ultimately, gaining self-awareness through psychometric testing and other assessments is the best strategy for becoming a successful remote worker, because it provides you with the insights you need to manage your time and routine."

*What strategies can someone adopt to avoid burnout when they experience too much time in virtual meetings?*

*Groom*: "Virtual meetings can be exhausting. Employees can sometimes explore alternatives to videoconferencing, such as a simple voice call, or they can agree on an email template that allows for a brief exchange of ideas without the need for a virtual meeting. Sometimes meetings are unnecessary or are booked for 30 minutes when they only need to be 15 minutes. My recommendation is to be strategic about video calls so that people don't end up talking into their screen for hours every day."

*Is there any other advice you can offer to remote workers when adopting this lifestyle?*

*Groom*: "Become self-aware and figure out your personality type, working style, anxiety triggers, and other traits. Self-awareness isn't a given. Most people assume they know themselves but are surprised to learn a lot more once they undergo various assessments. There are many approaches to improving job satisfaction in a remote environment, but they can't be successfully honed unless the person has a sound understanding of their personal traits."

## Strategies for Overcoming Loneliness

Experiencing ongoing feelings of loneliness can lead to depression, anxiety, and even problems with your physical health. Working alone in an isolated environment with few or no social interactions can easily cause you to become lonely if you don't actively take steps to prevent it.

In addition to scheduling time with co-workers and teammates to meet virtually for social gatherings and team-building activities, try to meet up with them in person whenever possible, for coffee, meals, or after-work drinks.

Because you won't typically be experiencing much social interaction during your workday, figure out ways to boost those interactions during nonworking hours. Instead of staying home to binge Netflix, leave your home for at least a few hours each day. Even if it's just to go see a movie at a theater instead of watching one on your TV at home, make a point to invite one or more friends to join you.

## 15 Activities to Help You Get Out of the House More

To prevent feelings of loneliness in the early days, work to schedule social activities outside your home. Here are 15 potential options:

1. Take walks in your neighborhood and strike up conversations with the people you meet.
2. Volunteer for a local organization or charity.
3. Participate regularly in some type of class or club.
4. Adopt a pet. If you adopt a dog, regularly bring it to dog parks and other places where fellow dog owners gather.
5. Participate in hobbies and activities outside your home.
6. See a therapist on a regular basis. If your employer offers an Employee Assistance Program (EAP), you can receive confidential support from counselors and therapists who specialize in issues like overcoming loneliness. These services are either provided for free (or at very low cost) by your employer or through your health insurance.
7. Go out to lunch or dinner with other people, even if you choose to dine outdoors. If you don't want to spend money at a restaurant, prepare food at home but eat at a park or other public place, or a friend's or neighbor's house. Avoid preparing and eating all your meals alone.
8. Don't spend all your money on things. Spend it on experiences that will get you out of the house.
9. Schedule more time to spend with friends and family, even if it's via video calls (during a lockdown situation).
10. Consider periodically working from a coffee shop, a shared work space, or another location where you'll be surrounded by people. Many remote workers choose to do this at least one day per week to break up their routine of working from home.

11. Practice self-care. Participate in meditation sessions, take yoga classes, go on regular walks, or visit a spa for a massage.

12. Get more involved with your local church, synagogue, mosque, or other house of worship.

13. Plan vacations that allow you to experience new places and activities. This will also give you something to look forward to during the weeks and months leading up to your vacation. Display photos from past vacations in your work space and as part of your screen saver to help maintain your excitement.

14. Spend less time on social media and more time experiencing life in the real world—outside of your home.

15. Plan at least one or two social activities per week and add them to your schedule.

If you have a flexible work schedule, take advantage of it and plan occasional personal activities during the day on weekdays. Also be proactive when it comes to socializing with co-workers (even if it's virtually). Don't wait for your employer to schedule team-building activities or companywide social events, whether they're virtual or in person.

While it's useful to stick to a regular work routine to maintain productivity and focus, once that routine starts to feel monotonous, you'll need to change it up a bit. Be mindful of how you're feeling every day, both physically and emotionally, and take steps to keep your work space comfortable and maintain a positive mindset.

When it comes to your personal life and career, set goals and make plans. Write them down and figure out what steps you need to take to achieve them within a realistic time frame. If you have defined long-term goals that you're continuously working toward, this can help replace feelings of loneliness with feelings of healthy excitement and anticipation. And make sure you have activities, social events, and vacations scheduled on your calendar, so you always have things to look forward to.

## Final Thoughts . . .

By now you should be able to see that becoming a remote worker can be a fun and rewarding experience that gives you more freedom and flexibility

## GET INVOLVED WITH PROFESSIONAL ASSOCIATIONS
## FOR REMOTE WORKERS

As someone who is entering or already in the remote workforce, you're not alone. There are millions of people just like you who are experiencing what it's like to work outside a traditional office on an ongoing basis. If you're not getting the emotional support or general guidance you need from your employer or you want to expand your social circle with people in the same situation, consider joining a professional association geared specifically to remote workers.

The Remote Work Association (remoteworkassociation.com/) offers networking and learning opportunities both online and in the real world. The International Association of Remote Professionals (iarp.pro/) also offers educational opportunities and the ability to earn a Certified Remote Professional certification. There are independently organized meetups held around the country for remote workers through Meetup (meetup.com/topics/workathome/), and a Work from Home Support Services Group that operates on Indeed (indeed.com/cmp/Support-Services-Group-7/reviews).

Meanwhile, on Facebook, if you search for "work from home" or "remote work," you'll discover dozens of Facebook groups, including Virtual Workers of America (facebook.com/groups/544818398895959), which has more than 200,000 members. Also, if you're a fan of podcasts, search Apple Podcasts or Google Podcasts for "remote work" and you'll find dozens of entertaining and informational podcasts, like Remotely Working, Digital Nomad Café, The Remote Nomad, and Remote Work Life.

while still allowing you to earn a living and maintain a healthy work-life balance. But planning and organization will be required to succeed.

You'll need to invest time and effort to enhance your written and verbal communication skills, along with your time management, organizational, and online collaboration skills. This will mean becoming more reliant on technology and becoming proficient in a collection of applications and online tools.

If becoming a remote worker is being forced on you by your employer or is necessary to protect your health, the changes to your work habits, workflow, and schedule will take some getting used to. Experiencing some trepidation or uncertainty is normal. There will be an adjustment period, but follow the steps and strategies outlined in this book to help you make the smoothest transition possible into this new way of working.

Finally, expect the technology you're now relying on to continue to evolve. Every few years, you will need to upgrade your computers, smartphone, tablet, printer, internet connection (and modem/router), and other tech. Meanwhile, as often as every few weeks, you'll need to download and install new updates to applications you regularly use, and then learn how to use the latest features and functions implemented in those updates.

You can also expect regular policy, procedural, best practices, communication, and security changes and mandates from your employer that you'll need to adhere to. In other words, becoming a successful remote worker will require you to evolve with your employer and the technology you'll be using.

However, you can also likely look forward to many positive changes in your personal, professional, and financial life, so take full advantage of these in a way that benefits yourself, your family, and your employer.

# About the Author

Jason R. Rich (jasonrich.com/) is an accomplished author and journalist. He's written numerous books covering a wide range of business topics and regularly contributes articles to several national magazines and popular websites.

As a journalist who specializes in writing about consumer technology, he currently serves as a full-time staff writer for Forbes.com Vetted (forbes.com/vetted/) and contributes tech-related articles to *AARP the Magazine* and AARP.org. Throughout the year, he also travels around the world and lectures about consumer technology, the internet, and digital photography aboard cruise ships operated by Carnival, Royal Caribbean, and other popular cruise lines.

For Entrepreneur Press, some of his recently published books include:

→ *Ultimate Guide to Shopify*
→ *Ultimate Guide to YouTube for Business*, 1st and 2nd Edition
→ *Start Your Own Photography Business*
→ *Start Your Own Podcast Business*
→ *Start Your Own Travel Hosting Business*
→ *Start Your Own Virtual Assistant Business*

As a writer, he's been a full-time remote worker (from home) since 1990, although he also regularly works remotely from hotels, airplanes, airports, and aboard cruise ships.

Jason R. Rich lives just outside of Boston, Massachusetts. Please feel free to follow him on any of these social media platforms: Instagram (instagram.com/JasonRich7/), Facebook (facebook.com/JasonRich7), Twitter (twitter.com/JasonRich7), and LinkedIn (linkedin.com/in/jasonrich7/).

# Index

CPSIA information can be obtained
at www.ICGtesting.com
Printed in the USA
JSHW021227141222
34822JS00003B/3